T0281315

iOS Penetration Testing

A Definitive Guide to iOS Security

First Edition

Kunal Relan

Apress®

iOS Penetration Testing: A Definitive Guide to iOS Security

Kunal Relan
Noida, Uttar Pradesh
India

ISBN-13 (pbk): 978-1-4842-2354-3   ISBN-13 (electronic): 978-1-4842-2355-0
DOI 10.1007/978-1-4842-2355-0

Library of Congress Control Number: 2016960329

Managing Director: Welmoed Spahr
Lead Editor: Nikhil Karkal
Technical Reviewer: Nishant Das Patnaik
Editorial Board: Steve Anglin, Pramila Balan, Laura Berendson, Aaron Black, Louise Corrigan,
    Jonathan Gennick, Robert Hutchinson, Celestin Suresh John, Nikhil Karkal, James
    Markham, Susan McDermott, Matthew Moodie, Natalie Pao, Gwenan Spearing
Coordinating Editor: Prachi Mehta
Copy Editor: Kezia Endsley
Compositor: SPi Global
Indexer: SPi Global
Artist: SPi Global

Distributed to the book trade worldwide by Springer Science+Business Media New York, 233 Spring Street, 6th Floor, New York, NY 10013. Phone 1-800-SPRINGER, fax (201) 348-4505, e-mail orders-ny@springer-sbm.com, or visit www.springeronline.com. Apress Media, LLC is a California LLC and the sole member (owner) is Springer Science + Business Media Finance Inc (SSBM Finance Inc). SSBM Finance Inc is a Delaware corporation.

For information on translations, please e-mail rights@apress.com, or visit www.apress.com.

Apress and friends of ED books may be purchased in bulk for academic, corporate, or promotional use. eBook versions and licenses are also available for most titles. For more information, reference our Special Bulk Sales–eBook Licensing web page at www.apress.com/bulk-sales.

Any source code or other supplementary materials referenced by the author in this text are available to readers at www.apress.com. For detailed information about how to locate your book's source code, go to www.apress.com/source-code/. Readers can also access source code at SpringerLink in the Supplementary Material section for each chapter.

Printed on acid-free paper

*This book is dedicated to my mom, my spiritual guru for inspiring
me to live, my mentor who always supported me
in this journey, and to all the weirdoes like me; I love you all.*

Contents at a Glance

Contents

About the Author

Kunal Relan is an iOS security researcher and a full-stack developer who has been working as security lead for Mozilla, Delhi.

He has published several research papers on information security in the esteemed *Journal of ACM*. Having obtained the acclaimed CCNA Security certification, he is also an Owasp ZAP evangelist. With his thriving experience as a security researcher and penetration tester, Kunal is known for actively reporting security bugs in a mobile and web applications. During the past few years, he has been working as a mobile application penetration tester and a security researcher in New Delhi. Currently working as a security consultant, he is the guy behind owlpro, a WordPress security scanning platform.

About the Technical Reviewer

Nishant Das Patnaik is an experienced application security and SecDevOps engineer. He is based out of India and is currently working for eBay in Bangalore. In the past, he has worked as an AppSec and SecDevOps engineer at InMobi and Yahoo. He loves to share his work with the community as open source projects and hence has been a presenter at Black Hat Europe 2016, Black Hat USA 2016, Black Hat USA 2013, and Nullcon 2012. He loves to code on Python and JavaScript. You can reach out to him on Twitter at @dpnishant and check out some of his open source projects at github.com/dpnishant. When he is not working, you can find him playing a piano or experimenting at the kitchen.

Acknowledgments

I would personally like to thank Apress for giving me the opportunity to write this book. This book would not have been possible without the support of Nikhil Karkal, Prachi Mehta, and Suresh John. You guys have really helped a lot during the completion of this book. It has been a long journey into this amazing world of iOS development and penetration testing, the outcome of which would never have been possible without you guys. The long journey of framing the whole series into a book was possible only because of your support.

Secondly, I would like to thank my mother, who has always supported me in all the things I ever wanted to do during my journey into the field of information security. Now, years after being in information security, it's a journey I loved and spent those dark and lonely nights with, days full of passion and zeal to discover and dive deep into this area of my interest. I would also like to say thanks to Sailmn, my beloved hacker friend as he was always there as a part of motivation in my research and was one of those few who understood my vision and my passion for all of this. We spent days together working on different information security projects and he has always been so good at everything we did. Also a big thanks to all the information security books you shared with me, as they were really useful for all the things I do now. I would also like to say thanks to all my friends, family, and my mentors at Mozilla: you are the reason for me being what I am. This has been an amazing journey with you all. Lastly, a big thanks to Jay Khurana, Kunal Mohan, and all other unknown strange and weird kids we see. I have a special love for all of them; it is really hard to adjust in this world and I feel the same as you do. Keep exploring this infinite universe!

Introduction

iOS is one of the most famous mobile operating systems in the world after Android, having about 28% of total mobile operating system market. Since its release in June 2007, it has evolved, and the current stable version is iOS 9.3.3. Apple has a stronghold of the mobile market, making it the second most used mobile OS in the world. iOS is a closed source operating system, unlike its rival Android, which is open source. That makes Android the de facto mobile OS for all other hardware manufacturers including Samsung, LG, HTC, etc. Since its release in 2007, iOS has been prone to jailbreaking; however, Apple has worked hard to make the security of iOS tighter with every release. They still have not managed to avoid jailbreaking totally and the current stable version iOS 9.3.3 already has a public jailbreak available by the Pangu team, which also claims to have jailbroken the latest iOS 10 beta. This leaves a big question mark on Apple about jailbreaking and other security issues being addressed.

iOS has always been a target of attackers, with many security breaches and causalities in the past, even though Apple has been very strict with its security policies and the App Store environment, which has a lot of restrictions on app development and deployment. Apple has also been very restrictive on giving up user data APIs to developers, and has denied a lot of Private APIs for use in apps, unlike Android, which gives its users data API like SMS, call history, etc. On the top of that, it has a sandboxed application environment in the OS that isolates the application from the operating system. Even with iOS's tight architecture, app developers still manage to make their applications vulnerable to attackers, due to penetration testing and reverse engineering in iOS. This is very different from the Web or Android setup, with Android running applications built in Java, which makes it easier to reverse engineer. This book will be your guide to working with iOS penetration testing and reverse engineering, and I recommend you go through each chapter thoroughly, follow the tutorials, and try replicating them on your end.

CHAPTER 1

■ ■ ■

Introduction to iOS

iOS has been around since 2007, when we first saw the iPhone, a beautiful device with iOS in it. Developed by the Apple Macintosh team, it was originally called iPhone OS, was renamed to iOS in 2010, and now runs Apple's iPhone, iPad, and iPod Touch. It is the second most popular mobile phone in the world after Android. iOS has been around for nine years and we have seen a lot of changes since its launch. It has always been in the spotlight for its security bugs, with the first bug hitting the web in 2007.

In this chapter, we talk about how iOS works, how it manages to keep away the malware from the App Store, and how the architecture of iOS is laid out. This chapter is an introduction to iOS and covers all the basics needed to understand the coming chapters. If you already understand the architecture of iOS and its file system, you can skip this chapter and move on to the second one, but it is always a good idea to brush up on your knowledge.

■ **Note**   We will be following Apple's latest 9.x and 8.x iOS versions; however, most of the features and issues are backward compatible and may work in upcoming versions as well.

---

iOS Introduction

iOS has been a popular operating system since its inception and its App Store has more than 1.5 million apps, of which 100 billion copies have been downloaded. iOS has always been praised for its user interface and is based on the concept of direct manipulation using multi-touch gestures. iOS shares Core Foundation and Foundation Kit frameworks with the popular OS X (the operating system in the MacBook); however, it has its own upgraded version of UIKit called Cocoa Touch. iOS also shares the Darwin foundation with OS X, which is an open source UNIX operating system released by Apple in 2000. However, iOS still doesn't provide UNIX-like shell access to users. At the time of writing this book, iOS 9.3.1 is the latest release and 9.x and 8.x are the most commonly installed releases in current devices.

Electronic supplementary material The online version of this chapter (doi: 10.1007/978-1-4842-2355-0_1) contains supplementary material, which is available to authorized users.

Lets dive deeper into how iOS works, including the security mechanisms of iOS and many other things that make iOS what it is today.

Security History

Apple has been quite successful in keeping the malware off its App Store, unlike Google Android, which has been tricked to host a ton of malware on its Play Store, harming millions of users everyday. The Apple App Store has managed to maintain the proper check on the quality and quantity of the apps on the store because of its long app review process, which gets annoying at times. Apple's app review process takes around 7-8 working days to review the app before uploading it to the App Store, which aims to keep the ecosystem free from malware. But it has been a blackbox game for developers, at least, as many of the apps often get rejected even after falling into whitelist categories, as Apple never discloses its review process. It just publishes a guide on making apps that can pass through App Store review process.

YiSpecter was one of the first applications to bypass the strict app review process of App Store. YiSpecter was the first iOS malware abusing private APIs in the sandboxed environment, and a recent study shows that over 100 apps on the App Store abuse private APIs, this taking Apple's security a step back, in failing to safeguard its private APIs.

■ **Note** Private APIs are not publicly defined and are supposed to be used by Apple only. iOS has many private APIs, including Telephony, Message, etc.

Apple has drastically improved its security model since iOS version 1.0, which had all the applications running as root user and had a bunch of security vulnerabilities. In contrast to what we see today, where every app has its own user and a sandbox in which it lives, the attack scope has been narrowed down to a great extent. With iOS 1.0, a vulnerability in any app could allow attackers to gain root privileges on a device's OS, enabling them to perform sophisticated exploits, as there was no sandboxing or any other strong security mechanisms. However, with its growth, Apple has introduced a lot of security techniques, making iOS strong and managing to keep malware away from its App Store through its app review process and strong security model.

Code Signing

Apple uses the *code signing* method to verify the authenticity of third-party applications, which is only supposed to be coming from the App Store and nowhere else. Apple signs off the apps on the App Store to verify it, and the kernel is allowed to only execute signed applications. All the pages in memory also need to be signed to run, giving no access to runtime modification of app behavior. Code signing is a very critical step, as it keeps unverified apps out of the App Store that may abuse private APIs. Unsigned code simply cannot run on a device unless it's jailbroken. For code signing while developing an app on Xcode, the developer should be registered and logged in. Without logging in, the developer can only test the app in a simulator.

Data Execution Prevention (DEP)

Data Execution Prevention (DEP) has been around since iOS 5.0 and is a technique to forbid arbitrary code from running in memory. DEP safeguards against exploitation by preventing code execution from data pages, such as the default heap pages, various stack pages, and memory pool pages. It is a way to distinguish between code and data, allowing only code to execute in the memory. Payloads that produce data over the network, files, etc., are not allowed to execute in memory. However, there is a workaround for bypassing DEP by using ROP (return-oriented programming), which reuses snippets of executable code that are already loaded in the memory to craft the exploit payload. Attackers frequently use ROP to bypass DEP. iOS tries to make such bypasses harder by enforcing code signing, which is done by Apple itself or by a trusted authority such as an enterprise that uses Apple iOS to distribute its private/in-house apps. This limits attackers from executing ROP, but not shell code.

Address Space Layout Randomization (ASLR)

Address Space Layout Randomization (ASLR) is an exploit mitigation technique used by Apple to empower DEP. ASLR randomizes the memory address of programs loading in memory, so even when an attacker finds a vulnerability he would still have a hard time getting the memory location. But ASLR bypass is still doable if the attacker gets multiple memory disclosure vulnerability. Hence, Apple implements ASLR together with DEP to strengthen the protection. The thing to note is that not all applications use full native ASLR provided by iOS, but by default the flag for using Position Independent Executable (PIE) support is available in Xcode since iOS 4.3.

An app is PIE if and only if the main executable and all its dependencies were built as PIE. Full ASLR randomizes the memory space for executable, data, heap, stack, library, and the dynamic linker (DYLD).

Let's simplify this attack to understand it more. Consider an application that can view a user's bookmarks and the content of the bookmarks, which means the application can read the memory address and memory at that particular point of bookmarks. The application can tinker with the memory address and change the value at any particular address, making the user visit web sites he never had in his bookmarks because of the existing ASLR. These types of attacks are not possible in current iOS versions, which use full ASLR.

Sandbox

Apple has been very particular and strict about its security, and sandboxing is the technique implemented in iOS. It is used to isolate an app in a container so that third-party apps are not able to access other applications or their data (including user data) or private APIs. Sandboxing enables iOS to lay out a granular control on its third-party apps, only allowing them to access certain functionalities. iOS uses the Apple XNU sandbox framework, which was initially called *Seatbelt*. It is implemented as a policy module of the TrustedBSD MAC (Mandatory Access Control) framework. Based on configuration that looks like LISP, it gets compiled into binary to be processed by the kernel. Sandboxing limits the scope of damage any malware can inflict on a third-party app, thus retaining the privacy of all other processes and files, even when the app is compromised. Sandbox rules are basic deny or allow written in the SBPL (Sandbox Policy Language), which very similar to that of a typical firewall policy file, and ensures only limited amount of permissions are given to the apps. For example, an SMS app shouldn't be able to access browser history and a browser app should not able to access passwords. The rules in sandbox take care of all these permissions. We will be discussing sandboxing in depth in later chapters.

iOS Boot Procedure

In recent years, Apple has greatly improved on the boot procedure of iOS and almost all the changes have been central to the security of its platform. It is very interesting to see how an iOS device boots up and all the security measures it takes before loading the kernel.

iOS has a very strict process of booting the operating system, where it checks for authenticity at every stage. When an iOS device is turned on, the processor executes the BootROM, which is a read-only and yet executable block of memory that's created during the chip fabrication process. It contains the Apple Root CA, which then verifies the signature and decrypts the LLB (lower level bootloader) and executes it. LLB then initiates the execution of the second level of bootloader called iBoot, after verifying its authenticity. iBoot in turn again checks for the authenticity of the LLB. If everything goes well, iBoot finally executes the iOS kernel to load the operating system. Apple initiated the main OS boot, so even before the main OS is booted, Apple verifies the authenticity of services at every step and ensures that nothing is tinkered with.

Once the main OS boots up, the kernel loads the system core services and iOS components and then the Apple native and third-party apps. The system services are loaded and the kernel then verifies these services one by one, whether they all have been signed by Apple or not. This whole process happens seamlessly in the background, once the device is turned on. It shows how particular Apple has been about iOS and its security.

Figure 1-1 illustrates the iOS boot procedure and shows the flow of booting up iOS in a device.

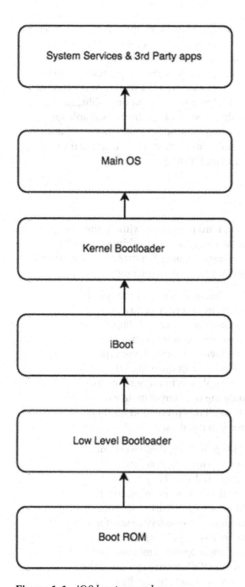

Figure 1-1. *iOS boot procedure*

Updates

Apple provides regular updates to its iOS through iTunes and through the over the air update, which can be directly installed in the device (since iOS 5.0). Apple also starts deprecating older versions of iOS as it steps higher and stops digitally signing the old version firmware, so a device running a higher version of iOS can't revert to an older version if Apple has stopped signing it. This technique is used by Apple to keep jailbreaks away from its ecosystem by keeping most of its users on the latest version of iOS. Hence, jailbreak developers and their users prefer to stay on an iOS version that has a jailbreak available, because jailbreaks usually take time to appear and then Apple releases a new version of iOS with the security fix as soon as it finds a jailbreak available. At the time of writing this book, the latest version of iOS was 9.3.1 and the last working jailbreak was available for iOS 9.3. However, iOS 8.1-8.3 had the most stable jailbreak available for iOS, developed by TaiG and the Pangu team, the two most active jailbreak communities. We will be talking more about jailbreaks in the jailbreak section and will apply the same techniques to an iPad for our further exploitation and testing.

What's New?

The rapidly changing world of technology is very hard to keep up with. At the time of writing this book, Apple rolled out iOS 9.3.2 and there are many things Apple has introduced in this version. Apple has introduced new security features as well as worked on the existing ones to make sure the user's privacy is always protected.

- *App transport security*: With the web becoming more prominent and the majority of apps becoming more Internet-centric, it is important for app developers to secure the network traffic of their apps from prying eyes. One way to achieve this is ensuring the app's communication from the iOS device to server is encrypted and the integrity of the data is verified at both the ends. To promote this security best practice, Apple has mandated the use of HTTPS in apps when communicating with any remote web server. Although developers can turn off this protection for their app(s)in Xcode, it is recommended you not do so.

- *Blocking installed apps detection*: Prior to iOS 9, there were some privacy gaps in iOS that allowed an app to gather the list of all currently installed apps; the first bug used sysctl() to retrieve the process list, which included the list of running apps. In iOS 9, Apple patched this bug so it did not provide the list of running apps to sandboxed apps. The second method relied on sandboxed apps being able to access icon cache (fixed in iOS 9) and the third method used the UIApplicationcanopenUrl method to open known URI schemes used by specific known apps using the brute force technique. This particular bug has reportedly been exploited by Twitter, futzing around 2500 known URI schemes, and has also been addressed in iOS 9.

- *Mac Address Randomization improved*: Mac Address Randomization was introduced in iOS 8 to disallow tracking of users through the network card's device address (MAC address). Apple improved this feature, which initially worked only when location services were off. In iOS 9 it has been fixed, this feature has has been extended to support inclusion of location service scans.

- *Six-digit passcode*: A passcode with a million combinations is harder to crack than one with just thousands. With this thought in mind, Apple improved its screen lock password to work on a six-digit passcode compared to its four-digit passcode in earlier versions. This doesn't make much difference to people using Apple Touch ID.

System Insight

iOS, as I mentioned, shares its design with Darwin, an open source UNIX operating system created by Apple. iOS gets its base from Darwin but it does not seem to be a full-blown UNIX OS to the average user, as iOS provides no shell access and limits access to the apps.

Darwin uses the XNU kernel, which is a hybrid kernel consisting of a mach 3 microkernel, some elements of BSD, and an object-oriented device driver API called I/O Kit. Darwin currently supports Apple's latest ARMv8-A 64-bit processors, including previous versions. The latest version of Darwin is 15.4.0, which was released in March 2016. Darwin has been licensed under version 2.0 of the Apple Public Source License and is classified as free software. This lead to many similar forks of Darwin and some open source communities aiming to make it better.

The iOS platform is made up of several layers, as shown in Figure 1-2.

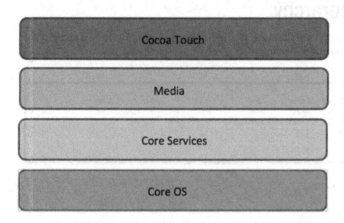

Figure 1-2. iOS platform layers

The bottom-most layer is called the Core OS layer and it contains the low-level technologies on the top of which all the other technologies are built. This is also the layer that directly interacts with the hardware. Apps leverage this layer when they deal with security or want to directly communicate with an external hardware accessory. It contains frameworks such as the Accelerate Framework, the core Bluetooth Framework, the Security Framework and the Kernel environment, such as networking, file systems, standard I/O, etc. It is the main layer of iOS, as almost everything in the OS uses this layer. Also, while developing apps, you need to use this layer directly or indirectly.

Core Services contains basic system services for the apps such as Core Foundation and Foundation Frameworks, which define the basic types all apps use. This layer also provides location, iCloud, social media, and networking feature access. The main features provided by this layer are peer-to-peer services for Bluetooth access, iCloud storage, data protection, in-app purchases, file sharing support, SQLite, XML Support, WebKit Framework, etc. You can find a list of all the features on Apple's developers web site.

The media layer, as its name suggests, contains graphics, video, and audio technologies to add multimedia to applications, which makes it easier to integrate media in apps and makes them look more beautiful and interactive. It contains graphic technologies like UIKit graphics and Core Animation Image I/O, audio technologies like AV Foundation, OpenAL, Core Audio, and Media Player Framework and video technologies like AVKit, AV Foundation, UIImagePickerController, and Core Media. This whole layer is all about the media and the frameworks available to make wonderful apps look and feel even better.

The top-most and the last layer, Cocoa Touch, is a version of Cocoa library available in OS X. It contains key features needed to create iOS applications that define the appearance of the app. It has high-level features like Document Picker, TextKit, multitasking, storyboards, Apple push notification services, local notifications, and it has frameworks like the GameKit framework, the MapKit framework, the UIKit framework, etc.

iOS System Hierarchy

This section takes you through the file system of iOS and explains the system hierarchy of iOS, summarizing the importance of each of its directories. See Figure 1-3.

```
Dungeon:/ root# ls
Applications    Library   bin     dev       lib       sbin    tmp
Developer       System    boot    etc       mnt       share   usr
DeveloperPatch  User      cores   include   private   taig    var
Dungeon:/ root# █
```

Figure 1-3. *The iOS file system*

Figure 1-3 is a screenshot of a jailbroken iPad revealing the contents of the root directory of an iOS device. By default, iOS provides no Terminal-like app and doesn't permit normal users to access the contents of any directory.

Let's now discuss the purpose and contents of these mentioned directories. They are very similar to ones found in all other UNIX-based operating systems, but with minor tweaks.

■ **Note** The iOS file system follows the Filesystem Hierarchy Standard (HFS), but still varies by name in some places.

Applications

The Applications folder is a highly sensitive folder that contains all the necessary apps to run iOS and is the home for all the native apps that come preinstalled on your device from Apple. These apps can't be uninstalled by a normal user and apps in this folder can only be deleted on a jailbroken device using a File Manager with root privileges or via shell access. Doing so can lead to unexpected results and is not recommended. The native jailbreak apps (installed via the Cydia repository) also reside here. The list of apps installed in this folder includes AppStore, Settings, Contacts, Dialer, Camera, etc.

Library

This folder is a tweaked version of lib folder found in UNIX-based folders, used as lib32 and lib64 to support multi-architecture. It contains all the necessary files and executables to be used by the user and the applications. Similar to other modern UNIX OSs, this folder contains shared libraries used by applications available for iOS. This folder has the following child folders:

- Application Support
- Audio
- Caches
- File Systems
- Internet Plug-Ins
- Keychains
- Launch-Agents
- Logs
- Managed Preferences
- MobileDevice
- Preferences
- Printers
- Ringtones
- Updates
- Wallpaper

It is a long list extracted from the folders inside the library and used by different applications and users.

Bin Folder

Like the bin directory in all other UNIX-based systems, bin contains all GNU core utils used by the system, which are basically the text, file, or shell manipulation utilities that come by default in iOS. On a jailbroken device, you can install more supported utilities if needed. A few utilities in this folder include bash, chmod, gunzip, pwd, touch, etc.

Dev Directory

dev stands for devices, just like in other UNIX-based systems. This is a read-only directory and contains hidden files managed by the kernel.

Lib Folder

lib is supposed to have shared library images that are used to boot the system and run the commands in the root file systems. However, iOS stores these files in /private/var/ lib and /System/Library instead. Thus, iOS lib is generally empty.

Sbin Directory

sbin is similar to bin and contains executable programs to boot the OS. sbin contains sensitive information and generally is available only to the root user on all UNIX-based systems. sbin is where RAM disks are uploaded and has important files like mount, fsck, and launchd for booting the OS. Deleting this folder or its contents may lead to a boot loop.

Tmp Directory

As the name suggests, this directory contains temporary files; the /tmp directory in iOS is a symlink to /private/var/tmp.

Developer Directory

This is an empty directory initially, but once you connect your device to Xcode and click the Use For Development button, the contents of DeveloperDiskImage.dmg are decompressed here.

System Directory

This directory contains the data of the root partition, specifically the frameworks in the Library sub-directory.

Boot Directory

This directory is usually empty, but may contain over the air (OTA) update data when available.

Etc Directory

This directory holds all the configuration files as specified by the Filesystem Hierarchy Standard (HFS) and includes important files like launchd.conf, passwd, and hosts. It has configurations files for Bluetooth, SSL, etc.

mnt Directory

This directory is not really used by iOS, as seen in other UNIX systems. It is supposed to be used to mount a temporary file system by the system administrator, but in iOS even RAM disks are mounted in the /sbindirectory.

usr Directory

This is a standard directory in all UNIX systems and contains static data.

var Directory

This is the mount point of device user/data partition and is symlinked to /private/var. It stores all App store applications, iTunes media, settings, photos, etc.

User Directory

This is the home for a default non-root user called mobile and is where user media and data is stored.

Private Directory

This is where /etc and /var are redirected, so you already know its importance.

iOS Application Overview

iOS has been doing pretty well when it comes to having apps on its App Store, with over 1.5 million apps and around 1 billion downloads. It's quite comparable to Android. iOS apps are written in Objective-C and Swift. Objective-C is the main programming language used by Apple for its iOS and OS X platforms and Swift has been around since 2014 as

Apple released its first version in Apple's 2014 WWDC. However, it does not have the popularity it deserves as a lot of apps are still being written in Objective-C. Developers have not made a move to this new language. In fact, even Apple doesn't seem to be using Swift much, as in iOS 9.2, only one App (the Calculator) uses Swift; the rest are still on Objective-C. Apple released version 2.2 of Swift in December 2015 as an open source programming language. Swift is compatible with almost every Objective-C library in iOS and is growing as well, but in this book we would be focusing on Objective-C, as it is the language iOS still works on.

iOS apps are built with Xcode, which is an IDE for iOS and OS X applications and only runs on Intel-based Mac, so to be an iOS or OS X developer, you need a MacBook or an iMac (you can also install OS X on a virtual machine). Currently, Apple is shipping Xcode 7.3 with Swift 2. iOS uses the Mach object file format, abbreviated as mach-o, for executables, shared libraries, object code, core dumps, and dynamic loaded code, which also allows fat binary files (a piece of code expanded to run on multiple types of processors). This contains code for multiple architectures, allowing Xcode to build universal binaries that can run on PowerPC and Intel based x86 platforms, including 32-bit and 64-bit code for both architectures.

Apple's current devices have ARM-based 64-bit processors, including the new iPads. In this book, we mainly use an Apple iPad mini running on iOS 8.3 (jailbroken) and iPhone 5 running latest iOS 9.3.1 (not jailbroken). App development on iOS is a pretty straightforward thing with not much scope of developing apps that change the way the device operates such as tweaks or extensions. Apple exposes very few APIs for third-party apps and, on top of that, the tough App review process includes a thorough check of an app's features, including a malware test. Apple's app review process is really effective. The fact that there have been only a few instances of malware slipping into the App Store speaks volumes about its effectiveness. The way such apps fool their review process is by constructing the name of the private APIs on runtime, which makes it possible to invoke private APIs in third-party applications. This makes Apple's static analysis of app review process vulnerable since it is not able to recognize private APIs being used by third-party apps.

Summary

This chapter was an introduction to the iOS and its workings, explaining the bits of how this operating system works. Understanding the core iOS will help you better understand the detailed issues in the coming chapters. In the coming chapter, we discuss applications in iOS and the development environment for iOS application development.

CHAPTER 2

■ ■ ■

iOS App Development Basics

This chapter takes you through the basics of app development and app architecture in iOS. This chapter is for readers who are new to this environment. Hence, those of you who are already working on iOS development may skip this chapter and move on. This chapter serves as a base to all further research and development in iOS. Topics covered in this chapter are Objective-C, Swift basics, Xcode basics, Cocoa Touch framework, simple user interface creation, MVC architecture, and more.

Objective-C is still a popular language for iOS development as compared to the relatively new Swift programming language, released by Apple in 2014. However, in this chapter, we will be discussing Objective-C and Swift with equal importance. Objective-C has all libraries accessible to Swift; therefore, we will be discussing the same piece of code in both languages for a better understanding. Objective-C is a mature language as compared to Swift, which is only two years old. Swift still has a lot to cover in terms of popularity among the developer community and the number of apps developed with it before it becomes the de facto programming language for iOS development. In this chapter, we create a Hello World iOS app using Xcode, and a sample malware-like app for iOS by abusing its private APIs.

Introduction to Objective-C and Swift

Objective-C has been primarily supported by Apple; it is one of the major languages used by Apple for its iOS and OS X development. Objective-C is a superset of the C language and inherits the syntax with object-oriented programming capabilities and dynamic runtime. Objective-C has its own syntax of defining methods and classes for providing object-oriented programming capabilities. We will be discussing basics of Objective-C, including its methods and classes that make it different from the C language. However, development with vanilla C and C++ is still supported. In the topics ahead, we discuss Objective-C as a language for iOS development, not its frameworks.

Objective-C Runtime

Objective-C is a runtime-oriented programming language, but sadly, it is often overlooked. Initially, when people start working on iOS or OS X development, they start with Objective-C because it's an easy language and can be picked up in a day.

© Kunal Relan 2016
K. Relan, *iOS Penetration Testing*, DOI 10.1007/978-1-4842-2355-0_2

Nevertheless, most of the time is spent struggling through the Cocoa framework. Understanding the runtime of Objective-C helps you understand the system and its workings better.

Objective-C runtime is open source and can be downloaded from http:// opensource.apple.com. Since it's a runtime-oriented programming language, it can decide what will be executed from the compile and can link the time to when it actually is executed. This is unlike its predecessor, C, where you start with the main function, after which it is pretty straight-forward. The runtime-oriented feature of Objective-C provides a lot of flexibility to developers; you can redirect messages to appropriate objects when needed and intentionally sweep method implementation, etc. We will see this in depth with the following example. Let's write a simple Hello World program in C.

```
#include <stdio.h>

intmain(intargc, const char **argv[]){
        printf("Welcome to C Programming Language");
        return 0;

}
```

When the compiler parses the code, it optimizes and transforms it into assembly. It links it together with the library and produces an executable binary. However, the same functionality when written in Objective-C depends on the runtime of Objective-C, which regulates what is executed.

Basic Terminology in Objective-C

Let's start with discussing basic terminologies of Objective-C and see how a regular Objective-C program looks. In Objective-C, a class has two parts—the interface and implementation. The interface is responsible for declaring methods and properties of a class while the implementation file defines the actual code that makes these defined properties and methods work. These two parts compile together to form a complete class.

Objective-C, being an object-oriented superset of C, uses square brackets to represent the object-oriented aspect of Objective-C, as a mark of differentiation of Objective-C from C. See Figure 2-1.

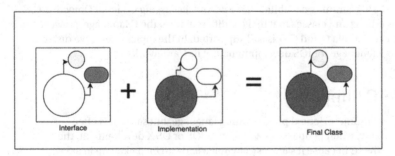

Figure 2-1. *Objective-C class*

A simple interface in Objective-C looks like this:
MyClass.h

```
@interface MyClass:NSObject{
        //Class Variable Here
}

//Class Properties here
//Class methods and instances methods here

@end
```

And an implementation file looks something like this:
MyClass.m

```
@implementation MyClass
        //Class methods defined here
@end
```

This example shows a simple class in Objective-C, with MyClass.h being the interface and MyClass.m containing the actual implementation.

Object Creation

Objects in Objective-C are like objects in any other object-oriented programming language; they have some properties and some behaviors associated with them. For example, a user can be an object and have properties such as name, age, gender, address, etc., as well as a few behaviors associated with it, like update profile, delete profile, etc.

Let's see how objects are created in Objective-C.

There are two main ways to create an object.

```
MyClass*nameOfObject= [MyClasstype];
```

This one is a more convenient automatic style, and it creates an autoreleased object

```
MyClass *nameOfObject = [[MyClassalloc]init];
```

This is a nested method call; the first call is the alloc method on MyClass. This is a low-level call that reserves memory and instantiates an object.

The second call is init on the new object, which does the basic setup like creating instance variables.

Data Types

As we discussed earlier, Objective-C is a superset of C, which means you can use all existing standard C scalar types like int, float, and char.

15

Objective-C also has some of its own scalar types such as NSInteger, NSUInteger, and CGFloat.

C-style arrays are also available in Objective-C, but collections in Cocoa and Cocoa Touch applications typically use NSArray or NSDictionary. These classes can only collect Objective-C objects, thus you need to first create the instances of Objective-C scalar types like NSString, NSNumber, etc.

■ **Note**   All the data types that hold a single data item are called scalar types, such as int, float, and char.

Methods

A method is just a function defined within a class (in OOP). Methods are used to organize code in small reusable chunks to reduce the work and energy and optimize the code and work. There are two types of methods available in Objective-C.

Instance Methods

An instance method can only be called by that particular instance of the class where it is declared; it's represented by a (-).

This is how a simple method in Objective-C looks:

```
- (int)addX:(int)xtoY:(int)y {
        int sum = x + y;
        return sum;

}
```

People who come from a JavaScript or Python programming background might find the syntax a little intimidating, so let's break it down to understand what each part of the snippet means.

The hyphen (-)indicates that this is an instance method. (int) indicates that it will return an int value, and addX is the name of the method. Parameters are specified with a colon after their names; thus, :(int)x is the first parameter, which is an integer named x. What is interesting to note here is the toY:(int)y, where toY is the part of the message name (think of it as a verbose label of the argument) and (int)y is another parameter.

Quite simple right? Yes! Objective-C is an easy language and it is also good enough for absolute beginners. Now let's see how to call a method in Objective-C.

Objective-C is based on the message-passing model, which is something like calling methods and some other goodies. It is similar to many other programming languages. In Objective-C any message can be sent to any object, and the object decides whether to handle it or ignore it In a language like C, it simply jumps to a certain location in memory and executes the code.

Class Methods

Class methods in Objective-C can be directly accessed without creating objects for the particular class, i.e., a class method can be directly invoked by calling the class name. A class method is represented by a (+) and can be called anytime by inheriting the particular class.

For example, let's add the following class method to myClass.h:

```
+(void)easyClassMethod: (NSString*)aModel;
```

Implementation of this method is done in myClass.m, as follows:

```
#import "myClass.h"
static NSString *_defaultModel;

@implementation easy {
...
+ (void)easyClassMethod:(NSString*)aModel {
        _defaultModel = [aModel copy];
}

@end
```

Now you can call this method such as:

```
[easy easyClassMethod:@"It's very easy"]
```

Now let's find out how Swift works.

Introduction to Swift

Swift was introduced in 2014 at WWDC by Apple. It is still a new language and is seen as the future of iOS development. Swift was open sourced in December 2015 and is slowly attracting more developers for iOS development. Even Apple is ramping up its app from Objective-C code base to Swift and not very many apps have been migrated yet, as discussed earlier. Swift is a sweet blend of Objective-C and C, taking all the best things of these two programming languages. Swift uses the same runtime as Objective-C and can easily run on Mac OS X and iOS. Currently, Swift has no compiler for Windows based systems but as Swift got open sourced, Apple has released a compiler for Swift on Linux that can be downloaded from https://www.swift.org. The latest stable build of Swift already comes in the Xcode bundle, which we shall need later to work. If you haven't yet arranged for an OS X machine or Hackintosh, now would be the right time to do so. After you become acquainted with Swift, you will start to play with Xcode and learn about app development basics.

Swift is an open source programming language developed by Apple and is just a better version of what Apple could take from C and Objective-C. It makes the syntax easier to work with. Swift has a simple syntax, good compatibility with the Objective-C libraries, and the support of beautiful Cocoa framework. Swift supports some really handy features like constants (which are variables whose values cannot be changed), fast and concise iteration over a range or collection, native error handling using try/catch/throw, and functional programming patterns such as map and filter, to name a few. Swift also has powerful versions of primary collection types—Array, Set, and Dictionary. Swift is made from C and Objective-C, thus, it has advanced data types like tuples, which originally were lacking in Objective-C.

Swift is a *type-safe* language much like Java, in that it keeps you aware of the data type of the value your code is dealing with. It makes the code easier to read and safer to execute. For example, when an if variable or an argument expects an int, type safety prevents you from passing a string to it, which also helps in debugging errors quickly and easily.

Swift Runtime

Swift by default uses the same Objective-C runtime, so it's fully compatible with all its features without any modifications.

Compatibility with Objective-C

In Swift, you can easily import a Objective-C library by using an import statement. The library support remains intact and is butter smooth.

Stored Properties

Swift uses the concept of stored properties to store data. A stored property can either be a variable or a constant. Stored properties of constants are defined by the let keyword, whose value, once declared, cannot be changed. In other words, it's immutable, whereas variable stored properties are defined by the var keyword, whose value can be changed anytime during the code execution. During initialization of the stored property, Swift provides it some default values through which the users can initialize and modify the initial values.

Let's look at some simple Swift stored properties:

```
var digit1 = 0
let digit2 = 0
```

Here, digit1's value can be changed during runtime as it is a variable; however, digit2 is a constant and thus its value remains the same.

■ **Note**   Swift doesn't require using semicolons after every line. You may need a semicolon if you need to write a statement that is multiple lines long.

Classes and Methods

Classes in Swift are pretty similar to how we deal with classes in any other language, and we can create a class in Swift with something as simple as:

```
class Animal{

}
```

Here, class is a keyword, and Animal is the name of the class. All the proceedings of the class goes inside these curly braces, just as with other languages, so right now, the Animal class is a fully functional class in Swift.

Functionalities or behavior can be added to a class in Swift by adding a method, just like we do in other programming languages. The following snippet is a simple example that defines a method in a class called Animal:

```
class Animal{
        varname : String?

        let gender = "female"

        //declaring some variables and constants

        funcanimalType() -> String{
                varanimalType: [String] = []
                if let name = self.name{
                animalType += [name]
                }
                if let gender = self.gender {
                        animalType += [gender]
                        }
                        return " ".join(animalType)
        }
}
```

So, that was a really simple example of defining a class and its methods in Swift. After defining a class, the obvious next thing is to instantiate an object of the class. The syntax is quite similar to many other programming languages.

Instantiating a class is very similar to invoking a function. To create an instance of a class, the name of the class is followed by a pair of parentheses, and the value returned is assigned to a constant or a variable.

```
let rocky = Animal()
```

Structures

Structures in C are very similar to classes, but they have a few differences. First is the use of `struct` keyword rather than `class`. Second, classes can be inherited but structures cannot. The third and most important key point is that structures are value types so they are passed by value. Here is the list of all that is common between structures and classes.

- Properties are used for storing values.

- Methods are initialized to provide more functionality.

- Initial state is defined by default initializers.

- Subscripts are defined for providing access to values.

- Functionalities are extended beyond default values.

Although there is a lot more to Swift, discussing all the programming concepts with Swift and Objective-C is beyond the scope of this book as we are focused on the security aspect of it. In this chapter, we discuss the basics of these languages, which should be sufficient to lay the groundwork for app development. Then you can start moving toward penetration testing of iOS apps. However, it is recommended to dive deep into iOS app development to get familiar with the app internals and their penetration testing and exploitation.

Now, let's hit the Xcode IDE and start to get familiar with the development environment.

Introduction to Xcode

Xcode is an Integrated Development Environment (IDE) developed by Apple. It contains a suite of applications, including an interface builder, debugger, code editor, and device simulators used for developing apps for OS X, iOS, WatchOS, and tvOS. The current stable version of Xcode is 7.3.1, which has the new Swift 2.2 installed. Xcode is proprietary and is used only for developing apps for Apple products, so it's available only for OS X and has no version for Linux or Windows. Thus, the only way to use Xcode in these other environments is through Hackintosh or installing OS X on a virtual machine. There are also many cloud-based Mac rental services available that provide online rental of Mac OS X machines.

Xcode supports a variety of programming languages like Objective-C, C, C++, Java, AppleScript, Python, Ruby, and Swift. Xcode comes with various iOS simulators (mimicking form factors of various Apple products such as the iPhone, iPad etc.), which helps the developers test their apps without requiring a physical test device. Nonetheless, behaviors like vibration and acceleration can't be reliably tested with a simulator and thus, it makes a hardware device necessary for development and penetration testing. Prior to Xcode 7, to develop and test an app on a real device, the developer needed to obtain a provisioning profile by joining the Apple Developer Program, which was $99. Yet, using some simple tactics, apps can still be tested on jailbroken device. With the release of Xcode 7, in June 2015, Apple no longer requires a license for deploying apps on the developer's iOS device for testing and debugging purposes.

Getting Started with Xcode

Xcode is available as freely downloadable software from the Apple App Store. Or, if you want the latest beta version of Xcode, just browse to `https://developer.apple.com/xcode/download`. See Figure 2-2.

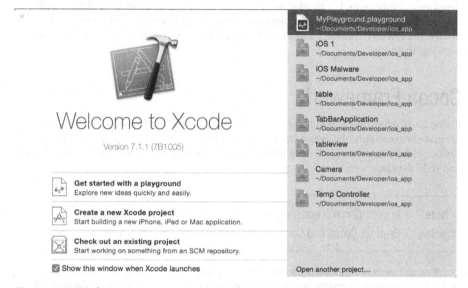

Figure 2-2. *Xcode intro*

Apple has also hosted its documentation on Xcode, iOS, and OS X development on the same portal. Although installing through the App Store is an easier and better way, just as with any app, you can download a `.dmg` to extract the executable. See Figure 2-3.

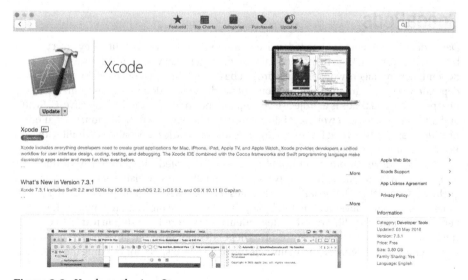

Figure 2-3. *Xcode on the App Store*

Once you have installed Xcode, you are all ready to start working on iOS, OS X, tvOS, and WatchOS development. Xcode 7 has an amazing utility called Playground. Try to find it in Figure 2-2. Playground, as suggested by its name, is a place of experimentation; it gives an interactive Swift coding environment, evaluates each statement, and displays results on the go. Playground is an amazing utility for beginners and for professional developers. Playground is a tool for testing small snippets of code without playing with the project code for testing new implementations and other experiments. Next, we will discuss the Cocoa framework and CocoaPods and then we will hit the ground and start working on Xcode.

Cocoa Framework

Cocoa and Cocoa Touch (including the UI, animation, and touch gestures framework) are just environments of iOS and OS X development. Cocoa Touch is a mobile version of Cocoa, which is used for OS X development, while Cocoa Touch is used in iOS, WatchOS, and tvOS development.

■ **Note**   The term *Cocoa* is generally used to refer to classes or objects based on Objective-C. Even so, Cocoa and Cocoa Touch refer to these two development environments.

Cocoa Touch is a framework for building applications on the supported platform. It provides you with an abstraction layer of iOS, the OS for the iOS devices. Like its OS X version, Cocoa Touch also follows the Model-View-Controller (MVC) architecture Cocoa Touch is the key framework for developing other frameworks, including the Foundation framework, UIKit framework, and many others.

CocoaPods

Dependency managers are needed in every programming environment. They are a bit different from package managers. Package managers can work globally as well, but dependency managers work on a per-project basis, meaning that once you install the dependencies of a particular project, you will need to install dependencies again for a new project. CocoaPods is a project-level dependency manager for the Objective-C, Swift, and other languages that work on Objective-C runtime, such as RubyMotion. CocoaPods provides a standard format for managing third-party libraries. CocoaPods is built with Ruby and can be installed with the default version of Ruby that comes as part of OS X.

CocoaPods runs from the terminal and is also integrated with JetBrainsAppCode integrated environment (a third-party commercial IDE that's available at https://www. jetbrains.com/objc/). CocoaPods automates the process of installing dependencies rather than making developer manually copying the source files, and it manages the versions of third-party libraries. The dependencies are stored in a simple text file, i.e., the Podfile, and Cocoa recursively resolves dependencies between libraries, fetches the source code of the libraries, and maintains the Xcode workspace for building the project.

Installing CocoaPods on an OS X is as easy as using the command shown in Figure 2-4.

```
kunal-2:~ kunalrelan$ sudo gem install cocoapods
```

Figure 2-4. *Installing CocoaPods*

CocoaPods has its own documentation and guide available at https://cocoapods.org. It explains the steps for installing CocoaPods, in case the first method doesn't work for you.

So by now, I suppose you must have installed Xcode and CocoaPods, which will help you continue. Let's hit the Xcode and start creating some basic modules

Hello World with Swift

After an introduction to these beautiful languages used for iOS development, let's start getting our hands dirty with Xcode. As mentioned earlier, Xcode provides us with Playground for all our experiments and code practice, so let's open Playground and start coding.

Select Open Xcode ➤ Get Started with a Playground. Then, provide a name and press Next.

Once you open Playground, you should see a screen like the one in Figure 2-5.

```
import UIKit

var str = "Hello Playground"                    "Hello Playground"
```

Figure 2-5. *Swift in Playground*

This is the default screen of Playground, and now we can play with it. Let's start by making a simple Hello World program according to the tradition, and then we can proceed to other things.

Hello World is really easy in Swift, unlike in Objective-C. All you have to do is remove the default code and type print("Hello World").

Let's try some basic conditional statements with Swift.

```
let age = 19
if age >= 18{
        println("Congrats! You Are eligible to vote.")
}
```

Conditional statements are this easy in Swift. Swift has if else, nested if and switch statements for all the decision making you might need while developing for iOS.

Now let's try some iterative statements before we proceed with making full-fledged functions.

```
for index in 1...5{
        print("\(index) times 5 is \(index * 5)")
}
```

This simple loop would run five times; you may check it out in your Playground. Iterating over an array in Swift is also this easy. Let's check it out with an example:

```
let students = ["charles", "james", "ricky", "jimmy", "aisle"]
for student in students{
        print("Hello, \(student).")
}
```

These small, iterative statements and decision making is required to make the powerful applications that we need. See Figure 2-6.

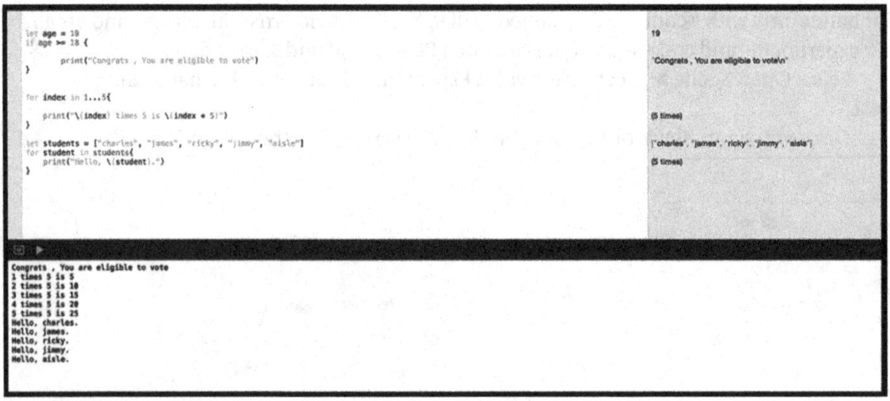

Figure 2-6. *Loops in Swift*

Now, let's create a function to determine whether a person is eligible to vote. Just as we did with an if statement previously, but this time the function will take age as a parameter.

```
funceligible(age: Int) -> String {

        if age >= 18{
                return "Congrats! You are eligible to vote."
}else {r
        return "Sorry,
}

}
```

Now let's call this function (see Figure 2-7):

```
print(eligible(20))
```

24

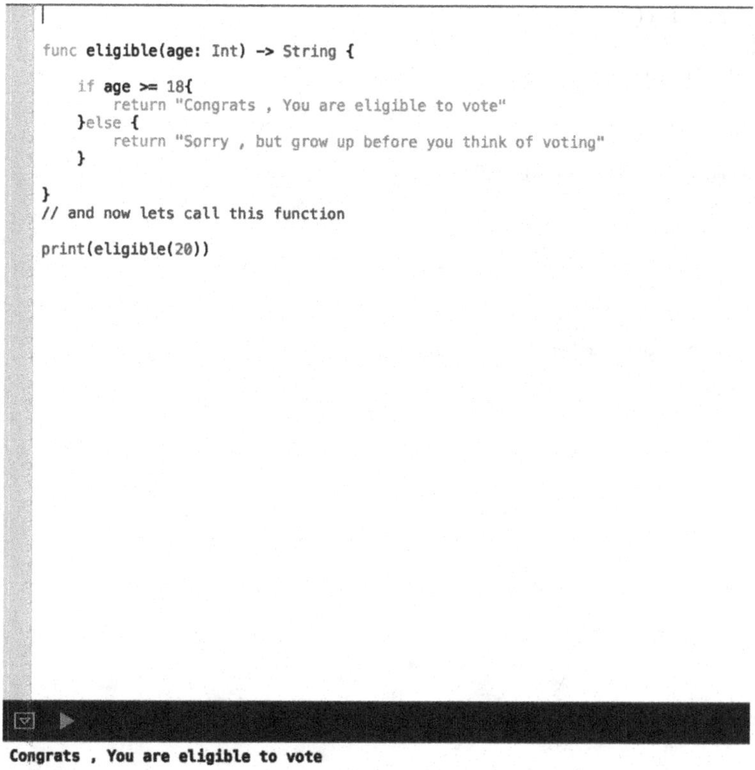

```
func eligible(age: Int) -> String {

    if age >= 18{
        return "Congrats , You are eligible to vote"
    }else {
        return "Sorry , but grow up before you think of voting"
    }

}
// and now lets call this function

print(eligible(20))
```

Congrats , You are eligible to vote

Figure 2-7. Functions with Swift

Implementing a class in Swift is also very easy, so let's try that as well.

```
Class ageVerifier{
        let age = 20
funceligible(age: Int) ->String {

        if age >= 18{
                return "Congrats! You are eligible to vote."
}else {
        return "Sorry, but grow up before you think about voting."

}

}
```

Let's work with the class now (see Figure 2-8):

```
let test = ageVerifier()
print(test.age)
print(test.eligible(20))
```

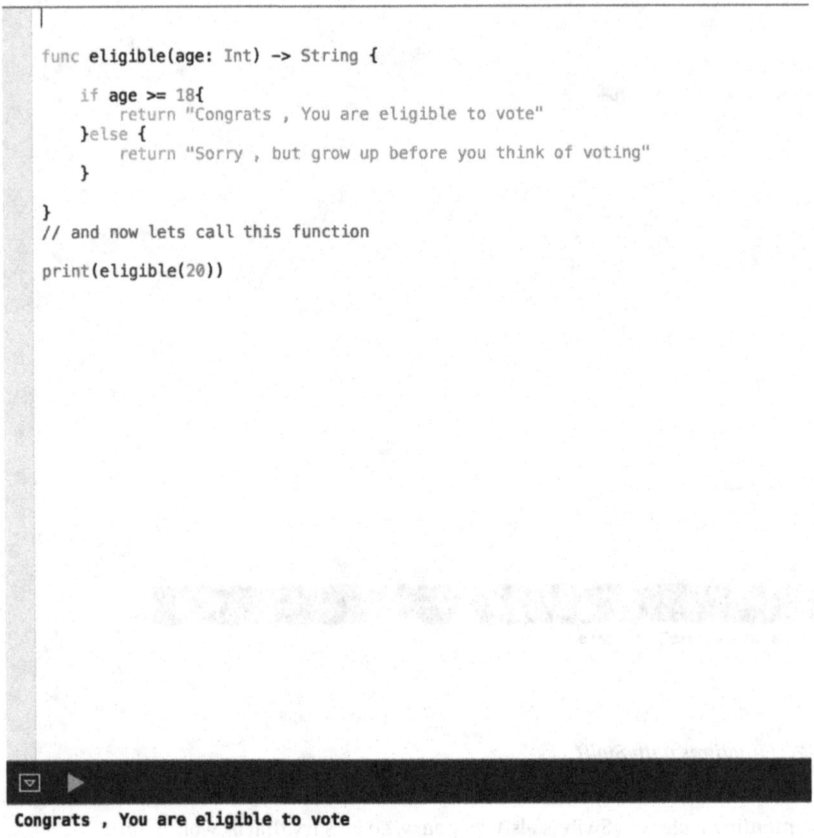

```
func eligible(age: Int) -> String {

    if age >= 18{
        return "Congrats , You are eligible to vote"
    }else {
        return "Sorry , but grow up before you think of voting"
    }

}
// and now lets call this function

print(eligible(20))
```

```
Congrats , You are eligible to vote
```

Figure 2-8. *Classes and methods in Swift*

Now, let's proceed and start making a Hello World iOS app using Swift. Close your Playground and start a new project now.

Open Xcode ➤ Start a New Project ➤ Single View Application ➤ Language: Swift. Click Next, as shown in Figure 2-9.

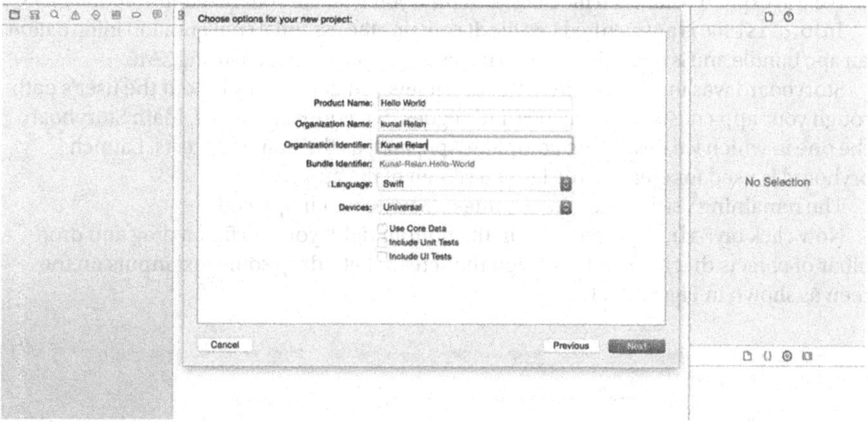

Figure 2-9. *Creating an iOS app*

Now, in the left pane, you will see a couple of files that Apple creates for us when we create an application. For first-time users, Xcode may look confusing, but it's actually quite easy to get used to. In the left pane inside the App folder, you will see a list of files, such as `AppDelegate.swift`, `ViewController.swift`, `Main.storyboard`, `Launch Screen.storyboard`, and `Info.plist`, and a folder named `Assets.xcassets`. See Figure 2-10.

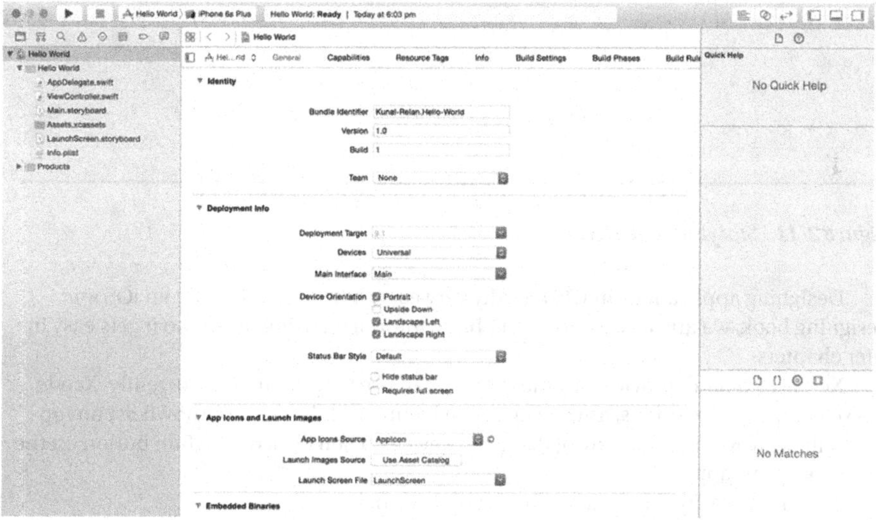

Figure 2-10. *The Xcode app main screen*

We will explain what each file does, and then you'll create your first application in iOS.

`Info.plist` file is a structured text file. It contains the essential configuration information of an app bundle and is typically encoded using UTF-8 and structured using XML.

Storyboard was introduced in iOS 5, and it lets you graphically lay out the user's path through your app consisting of scenes and segues that connect screens. Main Storyboard is the one in which we design the complete App, and, as the name suggests, Launch Storyboard is used for creating the launch screen of the app.

The remaining `.swift` files are the ones we write in our app code.

Now click on `Main.storyboard`. On the bottom right, you will find a drag and drop toolbar of objects that are used to design the screen. Let's drop some text inputs on the screen as shown in Figure 2-11.

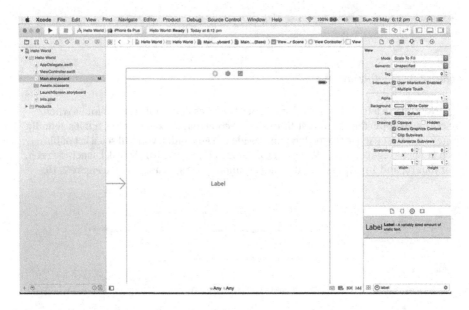

Figure 2-11. *Storyboard designing*

Designing applications in iOS is really very easy; however, as it is not an iOS app designing book, we are only taking a very basic tutorial on using Xcode, so it gets easy in later chapters.

Xcode by default provides a simulator we can use to test our app. Currently, Xcode has selected iPhone 6S Plus, as you can see in Figure 2-11. In the drop-down list on top-most tab bar, you can select any of the listed devices. Then click on the Run button on the side to test your app.

Now, let's use Swift to change the text of this label:

1. On the top-right you will see a button with two rings. Click on that button.

2. A partitioned screen will open up, where one side is covered by the storyboard and the other by the `ViewController.swift` file. Click on the label now.

3. Hold the control button and drag the cursor from the label to inside the ViewController class in the .swift file.

4. A dialog box will open up asking for the name. Provide a name for the label and press Enter (see Figure 2-12).

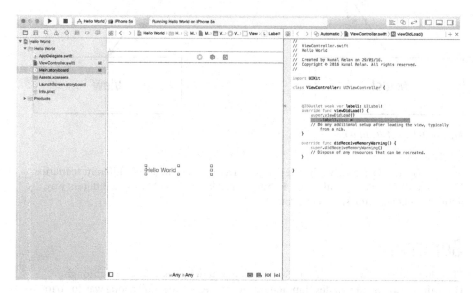

Figure 2-12. *Integrating label in a Swift file*

Now, inside viewDidLoad, write the code to change the text of this label.

Changing text of the label is pretty straightforward; all we have to do is write this code inside viewDidLoad:

```
self.labelName.text = "Your Text Here"
```

And that is it. Now, when you run your application, the text of the label will change to what you provided in the code.

iOS Application Architecture

iOS strictly asks developers to follow the MVC pattern while developing their apps. The Model-View-Controller (MVC) design pattern breaks up the app's code into three parts—the model, view, and controller. Each part of the app's code shares a particular responsibility and they integrate with each other in a particular way (see Figure 2-13).

- *Model*: Represents the business logic of the application.

- *View*: Represents what the user sees in the device.

- *Controller*: Acts as a mediator between the view and model just to break the direct communication between the two.

29

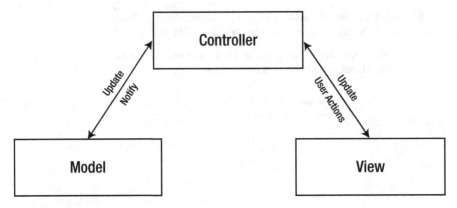

Figure 2-13. *MVC in iOS*

An iOS app may follow other design patterns as well, which suit different scenarios. However, MVC is a frequently used architecture. iOS has used MVC in a different way, although following the same concepts.

Summary

This chapter serves as a base for iOS app development basics, taking you through Objective-C and Swift app development using Xcode. There is still a long way to go to penetrate into iOS apps. So let's start the security part of iOS apps in the next chapter, where we will discuss common vulnerabilities found in iOS apps and jailbreaking. You may have already heard about iOS jailbreaking. It is very popular among hard-core iOS fans, so, before jumping into the next chapter, I suggest you go ahead and practice Swift and Objective-C to strengthen your iOS environment and programming concepts and techniques.

CHAPTER 3

■ ■ ■

iOS App Vulnerabilities and Jailbreaking

This chapter builds on the finer parts of your iOS security knowledge. In the previous chapter, you learned about iOS applications development. This chapter discusses the "whys" and "hows" of jailbreaking. We discuss how a jailbreak works on an iOS device and how to install repositories on Cydia. After jailbreaking, we will set up our penetration testing and reverse engineering lab for iOS security testing.

■ **Note**   You need to be running an iOS version for which public jailbreak is available in order to complete this module and do further testing.

Introduction to Security and Vulnerabilities in iOS

So far we have discussed iOS architecture in general and iOS app development. Now we'll jailbreak our iOS device and set up our test platform by installing our tools on the device itself and on a host machine, preferably a Mac.

What Is Jailbreaking?

Jailbreaking an iOS device is about removing any or all restrictions imposed on it by Apple. The primary objective of jailbreaking is to gain superuser privileges. It simply allows root access to the file system so that users can perform activities that were otherwise restricted, such as installing apps from sources other than the official App Store.

iOS jailbreaking has been around since iOS's debut in 2007. Back then, it was mostly popular among enthusiasts and hackers, and not so much with the average user. However, more iOS developers started developing "interesting" apps and tweaks/extensions for existing apps on the official App Store that leveraged the superuser privileges that would otherwise not be available. That is when the average user started noticing. Initially, people tried their hands at these tools just to make their iOS experience "different" from others. The most common reasons for jailbreaking the devices are device customization, unlocking carrier-locked phones, and software piracy. iOS jailbreaking is comparable to "rooting" Android devices, as technically both are a means to escalate the privileges over the phone.

Android devices are generally more customizable than iOS devices, as they natively support third-party app installations (outside of Google Play Store). Certain devices even allow users to modify their operating systems after unlocking the bootloader. So OEMs (original equipment manufacturers) even supply documentation for unlocking their device's bootloader on their official web sites. On the other hand, iOS jailbreaking is a relatively challenging task as there is no scope of customization without gaining superuser privileges. This means finding and exploiting vulnerabilities in the device's components.

iOS jailbreaking violates Apple's end user license agreement and voids the warranty of the device. However, in 2010 the Electronic Frontier Foundation (EFF) managed to get certain exemptions amended into the Digital Millennium Copyright Act (DMCA) that keep the jailbreaking community safe from legal prosecutions.

Jailbreaking iOS

This section covers the steps required to jailbreak an iOS device. At the time of writing this book, iOS 9.1 was the latest version of iOS to have a stable jailbreak available to the public. However, examples in this book use a jailbroken iOS 8.3 device. Teams like TaiG, PPJailbreak, and Pangu have released their public jailbreaks since iOS 8.

The TaiG team has the latest jailbreak for iOS 8.3, which is readily available to download for both OS X and Windows (see Figure 3-1).

Figure 3-1. iOS jailbreak using TaiG

Jailbreaking an iOS device is very easy; it's really just a click of button. All you need to do is install the tool that's appropriate for your version of iOS. You can find a list of jailbreak tools and the links released for various versions of iOS at https:// canijailbreak.com/.

You can follow the instructions mentioned for each of the tool's web sites to understand the steps required to install the jailbreak on your device. Most jailbreak tools are well tested to be non-destructive and non-intrusive to user data, as a precaution, it is recommended that you always back up your device with iTunes so you can restore it if any unexpected data loss happens during the process. Figure 3-2 shows how quick the process is when using TaiG.

Figure 3-2. *iOS jailbreaking*

Finally, you will have a jailbroken device for further testing purposes. The following examples and screenshots show an iOS 8.3 that's been jailbroken. See Figure 3-3.

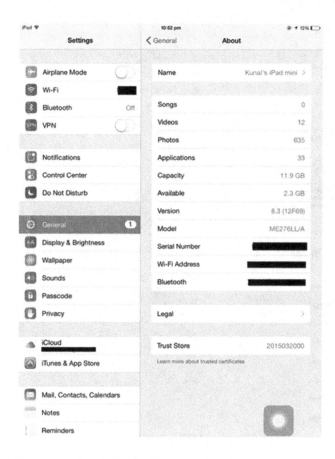

Figure 3-3. *Penetration testing device*

Once you have successfully jailbroken your device, you will notice a new app installed on the device called Cydia. Cydia is a repository (an alternative marketplace) for jailbroken apps and tweaks. It was developed by Jay Freeman (@saurik) and is the one-stop shop for all your customization and tweaking needs.

SSHing in iOS

To access the iOS device's file system or run a command on the device from a remote computer (say your Mac), you might want to install the OpenSSH (SSH means Secure Shell) server on the device. You can search the package on the Cydia app and tap on the Install button. See Figure 3-4.

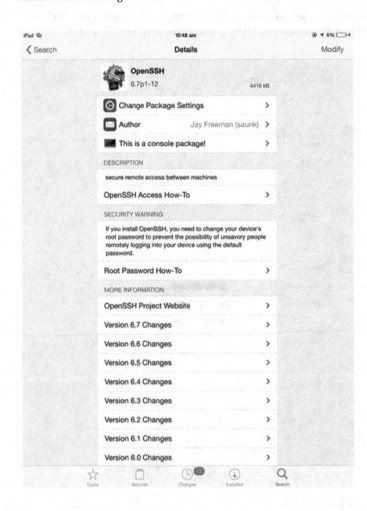

Figure 3-4. *Installing OpenSSH*

If you have a larger device like the iPad or if you are comfortable typing commands using the onscreen keyboard, you can also install the Mobile Terminal app, using Cydia to access the shell on the device itself.

■ **Caution**   The default SSH password for an iOS device is `alpine` and you should consider changing the default password.

Once you have set up the OpenSSH server on your device, you can log in to your iOS device using your favorite SSH client, as shown in Figure 3-5.

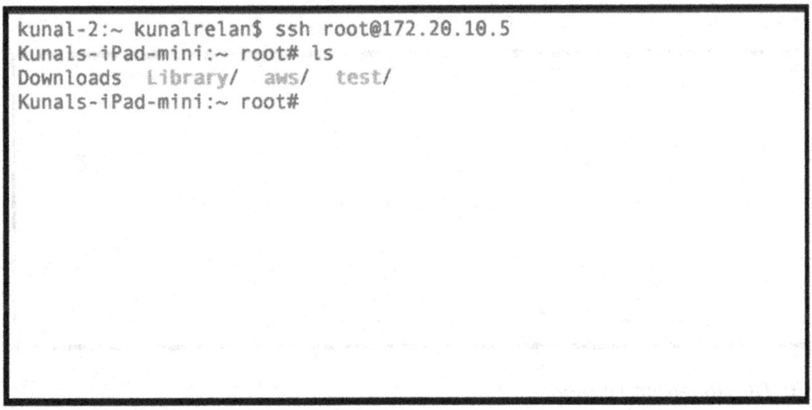

```
kunal-2:~ kunalrelan$ ssh root@172.20.10.5
Kunals-iPad-mini:~ root# ls
Downloads  Library/  aws/  test/
Kunals-iPad-mini:~ root#
```

Figure 3-5. SSH in iOS

In Figure 3-5, I have taken a SSH on my iPad. It didn't prompt me for a password, as I added my OS X keys in the known hosts of iOS so that it doesn't ask for the password every time I log in. However, in your case when you first log in to the device, it will ask you for the password. The default password is `alpine`, which you should obviously change after you first log in. Once you get the shell access, you may want to explore the iOS file system, as discussed in the previous chapters.

Installing the Tools

Now let's install some more tools on our host machine (laptop/desktop) to prepare our lab for iOS penetration testing.

Installing class-dump

The first tool on the list is `class-dump`. As the name suggests, `class-dump` is a command-line utility to dump the declarations for the classes, categories, and protocols specifications from the Objective-C runtime information that's stored in mach-o files in a readable format. `class-dump` is an amazing utility for looking into closed source applications, frameworks, etc., in order to gain insight into their design and make a fair guess about their workings during runtime. See Figure 3-6.

`class-dump` is only available for OS X. Installing `class-dump` is easy. Let's install it and see how we can use it for our purposes:

1. Download the disk image from `http://stevenygard.com/projects/class-dump/`.

2. Mount the disk image on any Mac running OS X 10.8 or higher.

3. Copy the executable into one of your folders where you want to keep `class-dump`.

```
kunal-2:~ kunalrelan$ class-dump
class-dump 3.5 (64 bit)
Usage: class-dump [options] <mach-o-file>

where options are:
        -a             show instance variable offsets
        -A             show implementation addresses
        --arch <arch>  choose a specific architecture from a universal binary (ppc, ppc64, i386, x86_64, armv6, armv7, armv7s, arm64)
        -C <regex>     only display classes matching regular expression
        -f <str>       find string in method name
        -H             generate header files in current directory, or directory specified with -o
        -I             sort classes, categories, and protocols by inheritance (overrides -s)
        -o <dir>       output directory used for -H
        -r             recursively expand frameworks and fixed VM shared libraries
        -s             sort classes and categories by name
        -S             sort methods by name
        -t             suppress header in output, for testing
        --list-arches  list the arches in the file, then exit
        --sdk-ios      specify iOS SDK version (will look in /Developer/Platforms/iPhoneOS.platform/Developer/SDKs/iPhoneOS<version>.sdk
        --sdk-mac      specify Mac OS X version (will look in /Developer/SDKs/MacOSX<version>.sdk
        --sdk-root     specify the full SDK root path (or use --sdk-ios/--sdk-mac for a shortcut)
kunal-2:~ kunalrelan$
```

Figure 3-6. *The class-dump options*

Using `class-dump` is as easy as choosing the right options from Figure 3-6.

```
class-dump [options you might need] <mach-o-file>
```

■ **Note**   Mach-O, short for *mach object file format*, is the file format for executables found in iOS and Mac OS X.

We will return to class-dump and discuss more about it as we begin pen-testing some apps. For now, let's move on to setting up the next tool.

Installing the libimobiledevice Library

The `libimobiledevice` library is a cross-platform library that permits users or apps to communicate with an iOS device using their native protocol to allow easy access to the device's file system, including information about the device and its internals. It even supports backup/restore of the device, manages installed applications and more without requiring a jailbreak, and works with the latest version of iOS to date (iOS 9.x at the time of writing the book). It is a very useful set of tools that we will need to communicate with our iOS devices.

libimobiledevice is a collection of utilities that includes ifuse, ideviceinfo, and ideviceinstaller. Each of these tools has a different purpose, including installing apps, syncing music, and more.

libimobiledevice is available to download for free from http://libimobiledevice.org.

Once you have installed libimobiledevice, you can run it from the terminal or command prompt, depending on the platform you installed these tools on. Since we are using macOS, we will make our terminal use this utility and fetch the device info of our iDevice.

```
$ ideviceinfo
```

Sample output is shown in Figure 3-7, where the sensitive fields have been censored. You can connect your own device and try it yourself to get a better picture of all the detail this tool prints out.

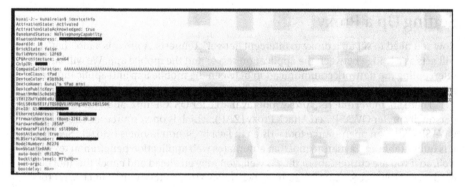

Figure 3-7. iDevice info

libimobiledevice is great for running forensics on iOS devices as well. It comes to the rescue when you need to get the maximum amount of information with the least amount of trace left on the device. I strongly recommend you install all the tools in the package and try them out before we start using these tools.

Installing Cycript

The next tool on our list is Cycript. It was created by Jay Freeman, the developer of Cydia, and according to him it is pronounced "sssscript". You may think of Cycript as a scripting language that has direct access to libraries written for Objective-C and Java. It is implemented as a Cycript-to-JavaScript compiler and uses an unmodified JavaScriptCore (Apple's interpreter for JavaScript) for its virtual machine.

Cycript scripts are more often used for hooking into processes on iOS (using the Cydia Substrate module) and modifying their runtime using a script that has syntax very similar to JavaScript. Let's install it on our Mac and see how can we use it to hook running apps and modify their behavior at runtime.

Cycript can be downloaded from http://www.cycript.org/. Once you download it, extract the ZIP. You will find three folders and an executable. This is all it takes to install Cycript on OS X. You can check the installation by running

```
$ ./cycript
```

You will be inside the Cycript shell (see Figure 3-8). Just exit using void exit(0) for now; we will explore this more once we are done with the setup process.

```
kunal-2:cycript kunalrelan$ ls
Cycript.ios     Cycript.lib     Cycript.osx     cycript
kunal-2:cycript kunalrelan$ ▌
```

Figure 3-8. Cycript

Setting Up a Proxy

Now you need to set up a proxy to intercept network requests. A *proxy* is a tool that will acts as a bridge between the application server and the mobile app. We will be intercepting the network communication between the mobile app and application's HTTP server using this tool and will check out the network requests at runtime.

There are many different proxy tools available for OS X, Linux, and Windows. I personally prefer OWASP Zed Attack Proxy (ZAP), which is open source and free to use. OWASP ZAP is an open source tool written in Java by Simon Bennets (Mozilla Security). It is quite stable and a mature tool that automates web application penetration testing as well, so if you are curious about that as well, you may go ahead and check this tool out at https://github.com/zaproxy/zaproxy/wiki/Downloads. It is written in Java, is cross platform, and is available for Linux, OS X, and Windows.

Another interesting proxy is Charles Proxy, which is a commercial tool that I will be using in the examples in this book. You are free to use any other available proxy of your choice, such as BurpSuite. They all function similarly. Charles Proxy is convenient and easy to use, so we will be using it. It also has a trial version that can run only 30 minuets per session and needs to be restarted after every 30 minutes, which is bearable for the utility it provides.

Charles is available to download from http://www.charlesproxy.com/. Once you download and run these tools, it is very easy to actually start intercepting traffic. We will further discuss this process in upcoming chapters.

Installing Keychain Dumper

Next we install keychain_dumper, which will help you dump the keychain database of an iOS device. If you are not familiar with keychain yet, you can find information about it in the first chapter. Basically all the credentials used by iOS are securely stored inside a database called the *keychain DB*. This utility can dump the DB for you so you can explore its contents.

keychain_dumper is available for download at https://github.com/ptoomey3/ Keychain-Dumper. It can be installed on the iOS device using the scp utility.

■ **Note** SCP (Secure Copy) is a utility for transferring files between two hosts. It is based on the SSH protocol.

To copy the keychain_dumper binary, we need to open our terminal in the directory. We copy the keychain_dumper files in and run this command:

```
$ scp keychain_dumper root@<iOS device IP Address>:/tmp
```

If the utility prompts for a password, type in your SSH password for the device (the default is alpine). It will copy the keychain_dumper into the tmp directory of your iOS device. See Figure 3-9.

```
kunal-2:Keychain-Dumper-master kunalrelan$ ls
Makefile          README.md          entitlements.xml .      keychain_dumper       main.m
kunal-2:Keychain-Dumper-master kunalrelan$ scp keychain_dumper root@192.168.1.9:/tmp
keychain_dumper                                                                    100%  287KB 286.6KB/s   00:00
kunal-2:Keychain-Dumper-master kunalrelan$ ssh root@192.168.1.9
Kunals-iPad-mini:~ root# cd /tmp
Kunals-iPad-mini:/tmp root# ls
MediaCache/          SpringBoard_reboot_flag      com.apple.timed.plist  keychain_dumper*   mobile_assertion_agent.log
RestoreFromBackupLock com.apple.audio.hogmode.plist cydia.log              lsuseractivityd.log
```

Figure 3-9. Installing keychain_dumper on iDevice

After you have installed keychain_dumper on your iOS device, you still need to do one final thing before you can use this tool. You need to allow read permission to the keychain.db file, which is stored in /private/var/Keychains/keychain-2.db. SSH will be required again into your device. You can then run the following command (see Figure 3-10):

```
$ chmod +r /private/var/Keychains/keychain-2.db
```

```
kunal-2:~ kunalrelan$ ssh root@192.168.1.9
Kunals-iPad-mini:~ root# chmod +r /private/var/Keychains/keychain-2.db
Kunals-iPad-mini:~ root# $
```

Figure 3-10. keychain_dumper permissions

Now we are good to go since our pen-testing environment is ready.

After installing a bunch of tools, you're ready to move on to understanding common vulnerabilities before we begin to test them.

Common iOS Vulnerabilities

No piece of software is 100% secure and perfectly secure software, has never existed. Security is an ongoing process and is evolving every day as hackers are discovering newer ways to defeat existing defense mechanisms. Every day, thousands of security bugs come up in different types of systems. Vulnerabilities are special types of software defects that compromise the integrity, availability, and confidentiality, in any combination, of the software. These defects make the application prone to being exploited by attackers with different motivations.

iOS, as we discussed earlier, is based on the mach kernel of OS X and so it has the same security features available on a Mac. However, iOS has another layer of security, i.e. sandboxing. Like all other operating systems, iOS isn't totally immune to security vulnerabilities despite so many advanced security features. Vulnerabilities are found in iOS apps due to insecure coding and not following best practices.

The following sections discuss these types of common vulnerabilities found in iOS:

- Buffer overflows

- Access-control validation

- Invalidated input

- Privilege escalation

- Insecure data storage

- Insecure transport layer

- Client-side injections

- Race conditions

- Weak authentication and authorization practices

Buffer Overflows

A *buffer overflow* is a condition that occurs when a block of pre-allocated memory (buffer) gets forcefully exhausted and is made to hold more data than it can actually handle. This results in unexpected parts of memory being overwritten. Buffer overflow is a very common software vulnerability and was initially documented back in 1972. Buffer overflows only occur in unmanaged code, i.e., software that compiles straight to native/machine code and is directly executed by the processor. The vulnerability is tied to the way the processor and native code manipulates the memory. In general, buffer overflow defeats the trust of the developer in the application.

Buffer overflow is a very serious and dangerous vulnerability, as it can cause your application to crash (to the least) and compromise data. Worst of all, it can cause code execution that can escalate privileges for a full system compromise.

A typical buffer overflow attack occurs in a manner in which an attacker finds a certain point of user input that's vulnerable to buffer overflow. It then inputs more data than the input can handle, leading to a situation of overflow followed by some payload by the attacker. All of this ultimately leads to attacker's code being able to execute in the program. Buffer overflow attacks are of two types:

- Stack-based buffer overflow (overflows in statically allocated memory)

- Heap-based buffer overflow (overflows in dynamically allocated memory)

To illustrate the workings of a typical buffer overflow, let's consider an example where a function reads your name and stores it, as shown in Figure 3-11.

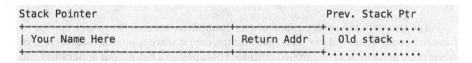

Figure 3-11. *Normal software is working as expected*

During a buffer overflow, the attacker introduces evil code in order to overflow the existing memory, as shown in Figure 3-12.

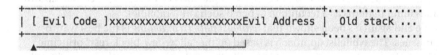

Figure 3-12. *Buffer overflow now exists*

So, as clearly depicted in Figures 3-11 and 3-12, it is a situation in which user input exhausts the memory space and overwrites the existing data (in this case, the return address), causing user-controlled execution of the code.

Memory is stored in two types of buffers—the stack and the heap—which is obviously where a buffer overflow can happen. As iOS applications run native code, they might at times be susceptible to this vulnerability.

Invalidated Input

Invalidated input is a dangerous and a serious vulnerability that exists in all types of software. As the name suggests, it is a vulnerability that exists when user data is not being validated and filtered. It is a situation when the developer accepts the user input and straight away processes it without any validation. Its impact can be very serious. User input should never be trusted blindly and should always be validated in context.

Since attackers can control user input, not validating such input is analogous to allowing anyone to enter your premises without checking their sanity or intentions. Untrusted user input can be received in multiple ways:

- URL responses

- Command-line arguments

- Text fields

- Files being uploaded by users

- QR codes

- RFID tags

- Any other source, such as any untrusted data read from a trusted server

An attacker will poke every option of user-controlled data and try to attack the software by crafting special payloads (files, strings, etc.) that are applicable in that context. So any entry point for user-controlled untrusted data posses a risk to your application and needs to be tested thoroughly.

Such vulnerabilities can be very dangerous and can lead to very sophisticated attacks. To prove this point, the best example is a jailbreak exploit based on one or more such vulnerabilities.

Validating user input is not so easy, considering the variety of contexts in which a particular vulnerability can be exploited. Many applications try to blacklist certain known malicious input patterns as a technique to patch such vulnerabilities.

Time and again it's been shown that *whitelist pattern matching* is the best way to fix such issues. The whitelist approach is based on the "allow-few-block-rest" principle where the legitimate inputs are allowed and all other unknown input values are rejected before they are processed by the application. You should always validate user input based on the following criteria:

- Specific patterns (e.g., phone number, e-mail ID, or URL)

- Data type (e.g., integer, string, float, Boolean, etc.)

- Null values

- Bounds checking (maximum and minimum allowed values)

- Duplicates

- Allowed character sets

- File (name, header, and size)

- i18n and L10n (internationalization and localization)

Using these methodologies, you can add one more layer of checks to your software for user input; otherwise, you never know when your software will be the next target.

Privilege Escalation

Privilege escalation occurs when a piece of software is unable to authorize the user, such as when the software fails to verify the things a particular user can access and unintentionally provides access to features or information otherwise only accessible by other user(s). Privilege escalation is a dangerous vulnerability that can lead to more harmful attacks, because it can give attackers access to restricted features of the application.

iOS jailbreaking is a good example of privilege escalation, where the purpose is to break out of the sandbox and gain superuser privileges to access restricted areas of the file system.

But in iOS apps, elevating privileges is not possible at the system level. However, apps that require the user to log in and perform certain functionalities may have this vulnerability in the way it authenticates the users and grants access to the functionalities.

Insecure Data Storage

This vulnerability occurs when a piece of confidential data is not stored in a secure manner. Devices themselves are never safe and all the confidential data stored on the client side (the iOS device in our case) is never secured and can be tinkered with by a normal user or attacker. Normal users will not always protect themselves against such things. If the device is tampered with or is stolen, the confidential data is at risk. Thus confidential data should always be stored in a secure manner and in a way inaccessible to other users.

In iOS, confidential data is stored in plist (property list) files or in unencrypted SQLite DBs, which again is a very bad practice. This vulnerability can occur at the server side and with a combination of other vulnerabilities that can be used to exploit and gain access to unauthorized data.

■ **Note** SQLite is a relational database management system contained in the C programming library, which is usually embedded in the end program rather than being a traditional client-server database engine.

Insecure Transport Layer

Insecure Transport Layer is also a high-level vulnerability existing in apps. All the apps communicate to a server in one way or another, so securing the communication between the app and the server is important. This vulnerability occurs when an application sends data over the network in plain text without encryption, which can lead to other serious attacks like a *man-in-the-middle attack,* which generally deals with the attacker intercepting communication between two people.

Network communication from a device to the server should always be secure and the security certificate should always be validated.

> ■ **Note** Security certificates are small data files that bind a cryptographic key to an organization's data and allow communication over HTTPS by ensuring that the client server communication is encrypted.

Client-Side Injection

As the name explains, client-side injections are when an attacker executes malicious code on the client side, which is a mobile device. The malicious code may come from different means of user data input in to a mobile application. In iOS applications, this is generally from SQLite injections, JavaScript injections, Format String injections, and XML injections:

- *SQLite Injection*: This one deals with improper handling of user queries when querying some data from the local SQLite database, and is a very common vulnerability dealing with user-supplied data in parameterized queries.

> ■ **Note** Parameterized queries force the developer to first define all the SQL code and then to pass in each parameter to the query later. This allows the database to distinguish between the code and the data.

- *XML injection*: An attack used to manipulate or compromise XML-based service or payload that can even lead to wrong data insertion, creation, or deletion.

- *Format String injection*: This vulnerability occurs when user-submitted data is evaluated as a command by an application allowing an attacker to execute malicious code.

- *JavaScript injection*: This vulnerability occurs on mobile browsers or apps rendering web views and thus occurs in UIWebKit. Most of the time, it is due to cross-site scripting (unescaped user input). This can lead to user input in the form of JavaScript to be injected and executed in the web view.

> ■ **Note** A web view is a browser bundled into a mobile application, and it allows a web application to be rendered in a mobile application. iOS uses UIWebKit for rendering web views in iOS applications.

Weakness in Authentication and Authorization

Although user authentication and authorization is largely handled on the server side, having the mobile application control parts of user authentication and authorization can be problematic, because it can allow attackers to escalate privileges using different methodologies. Common device features like unique identifiers are often used to identify users, which is bad practice and can be easily exploited. User authentication and authorization should be purely server side-based, giving the least significant role to the mobile application and using the fewest device features for better security.

Summary

This chapter discussed all the common existing iOS vulnerabilities and showed you how to configure the tools as well. You also learned how to jailbreak your device. This chapter builds on your understanding about the iOS vulnerabilities, which will act as your base for a deeper understanding of securing iOS applications.

In the next chapter, we discuss blackbox testing of iOS-based applications, based on these common vulnerabilities.

CHAPTER 4

Blackbox Testing iOS Apps

It's been a long journey discussing the ins and outs of iOS, including its security features, loopholes, development, and tools. Now we have finally reached the point where we will start testing our applications. In this chapter, you will be using all tools we installed in the previous chapters to test your iOS applications. We will also check out some vulnerable iOS applications by futzing with and exploiting them.

Note   You need a jailbroken iOS device to try these examples in this chapter.

Intercepting Network Traffic

The first thing we will be doing is intercepting the network traffic from the iOS device, analyzing the HTTP(S) requests, and modifying them when necessary. Intercepting network requests is a very important part of iOS penetration testing, as we need to analyze the network requests between the client and the server. This can be the phase where we might find some web-related vulnerabilities such as SQL injection, cross-site scripting, broken authentication, insecure session management, etc.

As discussed in the previous chapters, this book uses the Charles Proxy to intercept the application traffic. You are free to use any other tool of your choice. For intercepting mobile traffic, we need to implicitly configure our mobile HTTP proxy; however, you can do something similar using a network interceptor like Wireshark. Wireshark is a complex network monitoring tool and here we only want to intercept HTTP-based traffic, so it might be overkill in this case. Here, we will be intercepting our app traffic using Charles Proxy. Before proceeding, consider downloading a proxy tool like Charles Proxy or OWASP ZAP.

© Kunal Relan 2016
K. Relan, *iOS Penetration Testing*, DOI 10.1007/978-1-4842-2355-0_4

Before we start intercepting network traffic, it's important that you understand the concept of network traffic interception; see Figure 4-1.

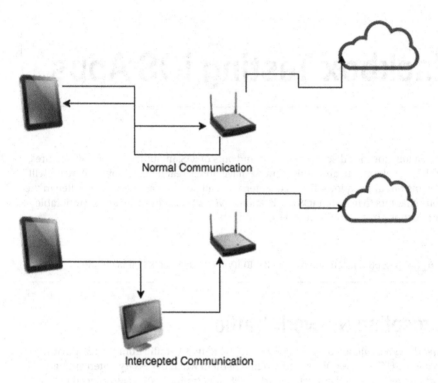

Figure 4-1. Network interception

Installing Charles Proxy is a pretty easy job and it is available for all platforms, as it is built on Java. Charles Proxy is available at http://charlesproxy.com/download.

Once you are done with installing Charles Proxy, you can configure it so that you are ready to intercept network traffic (see Figure 4-2).

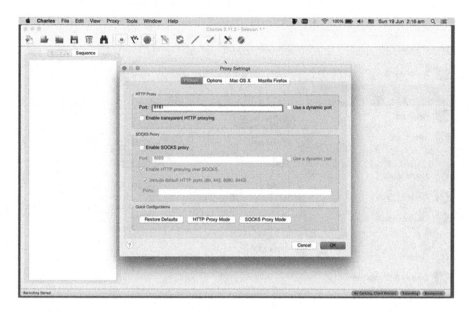

Figure 4-2. *Configuring Charles Proxy*

Let's configure Charles on our iPad to intercept app traffic. To do so, you go to the Proxy tab, then select Proxy Settings. Enter a port and click OK.

That's it! Charles is now configured to intercept network requests on your selected port. I generally use port 8181 for Charles, but you can use any other free port. Now you need to find the IP addresses of both systems, but make sure that you choose the IP of the same subnet to which both your Mac and iOS device are connected. In Linux/UNIX, you can print your IP address by running the `ifconfig` command in a shell. Once you have your IP address, you are all ready to set up HTTP proxy on your iOS device.

The final step is to configure HTTP proxy on the iPad and start intercepting, as shown in Figure 4-3.

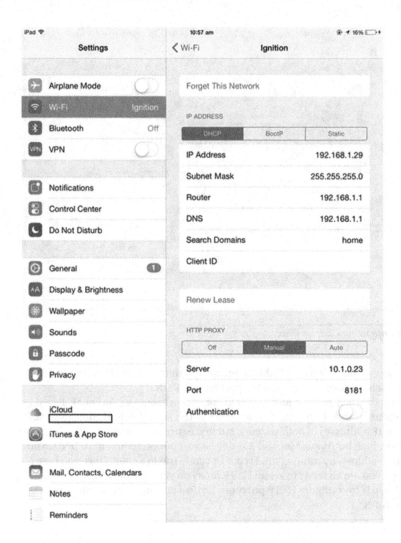

Figure 4-3. *Configuring HTTP proxy*

After you configure your iOS device to use your proxy settings, network requests start passing through the Charles server and you may see a lot of requests appearing in Charles (if the Recording mode is ON).

The last step in intercepting is viewing and editing the SSL encrypted traffic, but to do that, you need to find a way out to decrypt the SSL encrypted traffic as well. For this, you need to install Charles' root certificate on your iOS device so that when Charles Proxy generates SSL certificates for random domains on the fly, the iOS truststore knows to trust such certificates and the SSL protocol can function properly without any errors or warnings.

Visit the http://charlesproxy.com/getssl web site and install the certificate. Click Done, as shown in Figure 4-4.

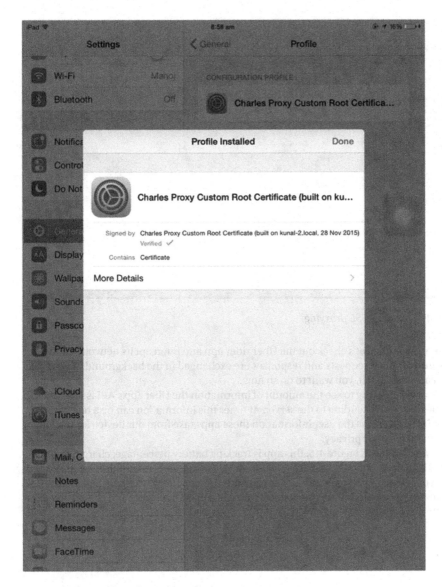

Figure 4-4. *Installing the SSL certificate*

Once you have installed the SSL certificate, you are all set to intercept network traffic, so let's open the mobile application. See Figure 4-5.

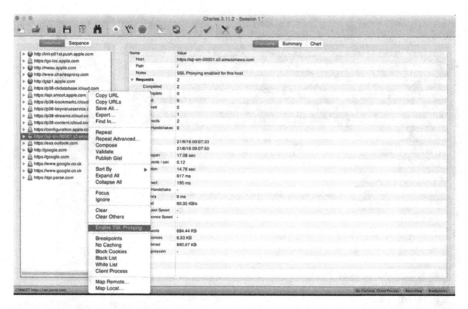

Figure 4-5. Charles SSL proxying

As an example, let's check out the Uber rider app and intercept its network traffic to get a sense of which requests and responses are exchanged in the background. If you have not already installed it, you want to do so now.

It's really amazing to see the amount of information the Uber app's API is fetching from the device and sending to the server. At times this information can be a real eye opener in that it shows the user information these apps take from our device for tracking us and breaching our privacy.

As you can see in Figure 4-5, this app is tracking battery percentage, charging status, private IP address, jailbreak status, etc. It is natural for someone to question an app's need to track our device's jailbreak status. You can add a breakpoint by right-clicking on the particular URL in order to stop the request from the app to the server and change the data midway. See Figure 4-6.

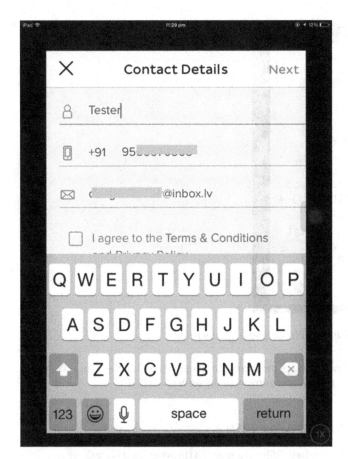

Figure 4-6. Network data interception

Defeating User Validation

If, by now, you are wondering what you can do when you intercept an app's network traffic, you should know that the possibilities are limitless and it is therefore a vital part of the penetration-testing process.

Let's install another app—this time a popular Indian food ordering app—and try to see its login and signup procedure using Charles Proxy. We will try to see if we can bypass the user-validation process. As I start the app, it shows the login/signup screen; the signup screen looks pretty similar to most mobile apps these days (see Figure 4-7).

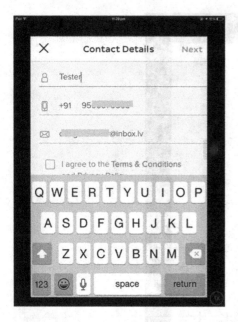

Figure 4-7. *Client-side validation is particularly vulnerable*

Let's fill in the form and intercept the form signup request on Charles Proxy. We will try our hands at modifying the request midway to the server.

Damn Vulnerable iOS App: DVIA

Instead of trying our newly acquired skills on a real app (to avoid legal issues), we need an app that is designed for learning purposes and has common and real-world vulnerabilities to hone our skills. Exactly for this purpose, there is a popular app called Damn Vulnerable iOS application (DVIA). You can download DVIA from http:// damnvulnerableiosapp.com/ or, if you want your own build, you can get its source code from https://github.com/prateek147/DVIA. After installing DVIA, let's open the DVIA app and start finding some vulnerabilities. See Figure 4-8.

Figure 4-8. DVIA

DVIA covers all the top iOS vulnerabilities), which we will discuss one by one.

Insecure Data Storage

This is a vulnerability that occurs when the application stores private data locally without proper security configuration, such as plist files, NSUserDefaults, Keychain, Core Data, and WebKit.

Plist stands for *property list*. A plist is actually an XML file with a .plist extension. Every application bundle has an Info.plist file with various keys and values that store configuration data for proper functioning of the app. Developers often store sensitive info in these plist files, as they find them quite easy to use.

Let's check out an app's Info.plist and see the sort of data that's stored in them. To view or edit these files, you either log in to the jailbroken device via SSH or browse the file directly on the device using a file system browser like iFile, which can be installed on jailbroken devices through Cydia.

All your app bundles are stored under:

```
/var/mobile/Containers/Bundle/Application
```

In this directory, you will see a lot of folders with long UUID (universally unique identifier) style names. These are the application bundle identifiers of every application installed on the device. If you browse inside them, you will find a directory with the same name as the app and ending with .app. Inside that, you'll find the Info.plist file, which can be viewed using the Property List Viewer component of iFile (see Figure 4-9).

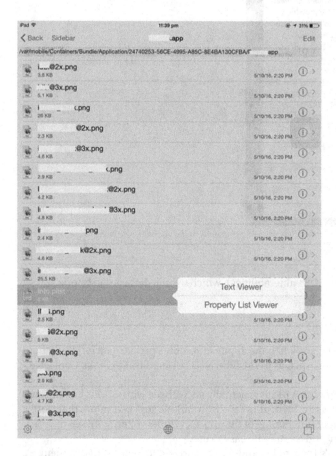

Figure 4-9. *Reading plist files*

As you go through plist files of iOS apps, you'll be amazed to find how much private data, such as credentials etc., is stored in them, even in cleartext. This makes it vulnerable to be read by anyone. In fact, while searching for examples for this book, I found a "famous" app storing confidential API keys in the Info.plist files, as shown in Figure 4-10.

Figure 4-10. *Plist file*

As you can see, this is indeed a real-world and popular app that is storing all its private data in a `Info.plist` file.

You can try to get your hands dirty on other apps out there and see what private information you can find by reading such `plist` files.

NSUserDefaults Private Data

The `NSUserDefaults` class provides a programmatic interface for interacting with the defaults system, which allows an application to customize its behavior to match the user's preference.

A lot of applications store user data in `NSUserDefaults` and this data persists even when users rerun the app. `NSUserDefaults` lets users store 100KB of data. However, a lot of developers use `NSUserDefaults` to save private data, which is generally a bad practice, as `NSUserDefaults` data can be easily read in the file system. Let's check out where we can find user confidential data saved using `NSUserDefaults`.

App data is generally stored in /var/mobile/containers/Data/Application/ <appId> and NSUserDefaults is located inside the Library/Preferences/ directory of the app data bundle. Let's go ahead and check out the Preferences directory of different apps and see the private data they store in the NSUserDefaults data store (see Figure 4-11).

Figure 4-11. NSUserDefaults

As you can see in Figure 4-11, a famous ecommerce app is saving a lot of user data in NSUserDefaults in plaintext. As you no doubt understand by now, on a jailbroken device this information is pretty easy to access. Hence, appropriate judgment is required to decide what data should be stored in such locations.

Dumping iOS Keychain

iOS lets you save your confidential data in something called the *keychain*. Keychain is a secure storage container that lets you save any data that is highly sensitive and secret in nature, such as credentials, API tokens, PII, and credit card information, in a secure manner. Keychain uses 256-bit AES encryption to store and transmit the secured data. Keychain natively is a SQLite database saved at /private/var/Keychains/keychain-2.db and data stored in the keychain isn't the part of sandbox scope. That data can be shared among apps using keychain access groups. In other words, if there are different apps developed by the same developer and the developer wants his apps to share the credentials or tokens to be shared by all his apps, he can do so by making his apps part of the same keychain access group during development.

On a jailbroken device, it is possible to dump the keychain database and view its contents. That may include your WiFi passwords, VPN credentials, app data, etc.

To dump a keychain, you can use a utility we've discussed in previous chapters, called keychain-dumper. It's available for download at https://github.com/ptoomey3/Keychain-Dumper, so just download this utility from the link. Inside the folder, you will find the keychain_dumper executable (see Figure 4-12).

```
kunal-2:Keychain-Dumper-master kunalrelan$ ls
Makefile                  README.md              entitlements.xml        keychain_dumper       main.m
kunal-2:Keychain-Dumper-master kunalrelan$ sftp root@192.168.1.4
root@192.168.1.4's password:
Connected to 192.168.1.4.
sftp> cd /tmp
sftp> put keychain_dumper
Uploading keychain_dumper to /private/var/tmp/keychain_dumper
keychain_dumper
```

Figure 4-12. Installing keychain_dumper

Once you have set up the keychain, all you have do to run keychain_dumper is use this command:

```
./keychain_dumper -a
```

where -a instructs the keychain_dumper to dump all the data saved in the keychain, including certificates, credentials, etc. (see Figure 4-13).

```
kunal-2:Keychain-Dumper-master kunalrelan$ ssh root@192.168.1.4
root@192.168.1.4's password:
Kunals-iPad-mini:~ root# cd /tmp
Kunals-iPad-mini:/tmp root# chmod a+x keychain_dumper
Kunals-iPad-mini:/tmp root# chmod +r /private/var/Keychains/keychain-2.db
Kunals-iPad-mini:/tmp root# ./keychain_dumper -h
Usage: keychain_dumper [-e]|[-h]|[[-agnick]
<no flags>: Dump Password Keychain Items (Generic Password, Internet Passwords)
-a: Dump All Keychain Items (Generic Passwords, Internet Passwords, Identities, Certificates, and Keys)
-e: Dump Entitlements
-g: Dump Generic Passwords
-n: Dump Internet Passwords
-i: Dump Identities
-c: Dump Certificates
-k: Dump Keys
Kunals-iPad-mini:/tmp root#
Kunals-iPad-mini:/tmp root# ./keychain_dumper -a
Generic Password
----------------
Service: BluetoothGlobal
Account: Identity Root
Entitlement Group: apple
Label: (null)
Generic Field: (null)
Keychain Data: <?xml version="1.0" encoding="UTF-8"?>
<!DOCTYPE plist PUBLIC "-//Apple//DTD PLIST 1.0//EN" "http://www.apple.com/DTDs/PropertyList-1.0.dtd">
<plist version="1.0">
<dict>
        <key>KEY</key>
        <data>
        ████████████████████████
        </data>
</dict>
</plist>


Generic Password
----------------
Service: BluetoothGlobal
Account: Encryption Root
Entitlement Group: apple
Label: (null)
Generic Field: (null)
Keychain Data: <?xml version="1.0" encoding="UTF-8"?>
<!DOCTYPE plist PUBLIC "-//Apple//DTD PLIST 1.0//EN" "http://www.apple.com/DTDs/PropertyList-1.0.dtd">
<plist version="1.0">
<dict>
        <key>KEY</key>
        <data>
        ████████████████████
        </data>
</dict>
```

Figure 4-13. *Dumping the keychain*

Once you dump the keychain, you have a lot in your hand you can work with, Keychain has all the confidential data stored in your device and you can easily dump all of that data with a very small utility tool and check out all your data in your keychain.

Although keychain is supposed to be a secured data storage feature, once a device has been jailbroken, the data in the keychain can be dumped and manipulated. Therefore, it's not a really good place to store user confidential data. See Figure 4-14.

```
Generic Password
----------------
Service: com.helpshift.data
Account: lastLoggedInIdentifier
Entitlement Group: ███████████████
Label: (null)
Generic Field: (null)
Keychain Data: (null)

Generic Password
----------------
Service: AirPort
Account: ████
Entitlement Group: apple
Label: (null)
Generic Field: (null)
Keychain Data: ████████████

Generic Password
----------------
Service: ids
Account: personal-public-key-cache
Entitlement Group: ichat
Label: (null)
Generic Field: (null)
Keychain Data: (null)

Generic Password
----------------
Service: ids
Account: personal-session-token-cache
Entitlement Group: ichat
Label: (null)
Generic Field: (null)
Keychain Data: (null)

Generic Password
----------------
Service: <636f6d2e 6170706c 652e5465 7374466c 69676874 2e76656e 646f7249 44>
Account: <76656e64 ███████████
Entitlement Group: VT6C486PNU.com.apple.TestFlight
Label: (null)
Generic Field: (null)
Keychain Data: ████████████████████

Generic Password
----------------
Service: <636f6d2e 6170706c 652e6f61 7369732e 6b657963 6861696e>
Account: <35323434 ██████████████
Entitlement Group: VT6C486PNU.com.apple.TestFlight
Label: (null)
Generic Field: (null)
Keychain Data: █████████████████████
```

Figure 4-14. *Keychain dumping reveals confidential data*

Performing Runtime Analysis

iOS apps are built using Objective-C, which is an object-oriented programming language. Static analysis of Objective-C apps might be difficult for security testers who do not have enough programming experience with Objective-C or when the source code of the app is not available. This is why inspecting the Objective-C runtime is a very interesting part for attackers as it has a huge scope of being tampered and enabling an attacker to be able to modify the behavior or functionality of an iOS app on a jailbroken device.

The Objective-C runtime environment provides a lot of opportunities for us to manipulate an app during runtime. Runtime analysis can be done by introducing a static library with these functionalities, but this can be only done for your own app during development. However, for runtime analysis of other apps, you need a jailbroken device and need to inject an on-the-fly interpreter for manipulations.

Cycript is an advanced method *swizzling* library that helps us hook into a running process and modify its runtime. Cycript is a great blend of Objective-C and JavaScript. Cycript provides an interactive console (REPL) when hooking into an application to control its runtime. Next, we will pick an app and hook its runtime to modify some of its content.

■ **Note** *Method swizzling* is the process of changing the implementation of an existing selector. It's a technique made possible by the fact that method invocations in Objective-C can be changed at runtime, by changing how selectors are mapped to underlying functions in a class's dispatch table.

Since we have already installed Cycript in the previous chapter, we'll open up our arsenal and start using Cycript.

For the purposes of demonstration, I installed the Yahoo! Weather application, downloaded from App Store. We will now SSH into the device and find the process ID of the app so that we can tell Cycript to hook that process (see Figure 4-15).

Figure 4-15. Finding the process ID

Once we know the process ID we need to hook, we can use the following command to begin the process:

```
Kunals-iPad-mini:~ root# cycript -p 802
```

This will open the Cycript shell, which should look something like Figure 4-16.

```
[Kunals-iPad-mini:~ root# cycript -p 802
cy#
cy#
```

Figure 4-16. *Cycript shell*

If everything goes well, you can check out the instance of the application by typing [UIApplication sharedApplication].

So as mentioned earlier, Cycript is a blend of JavaScript and Objective-C. You can confirm yourself if you see that I assigned a variable in JavaScript syntax and the value is actually the singleton instance of the application (see Figure 4-17).

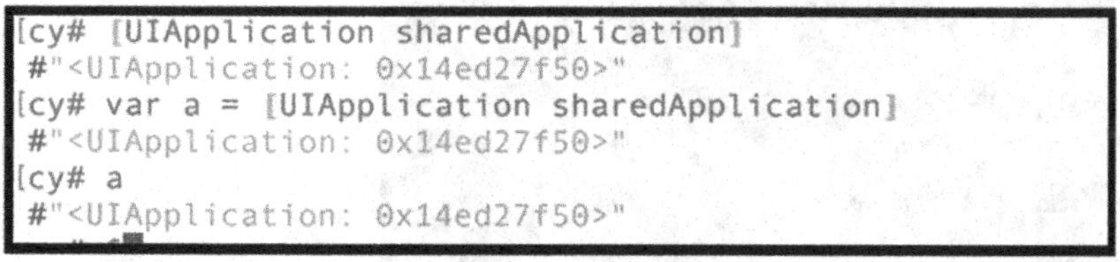

```
[cy# [UIApplication sharedApplication]
#"<UIApplication: 0x14ed27f50>"
[cy# var a = [UIApplication sharedApplication]
#"<UIApplication: 0x14ed27f50>"
[cy# a
#"<UIApplication: 0x14ed27f50>"
```

Figure 4-17. *Instance of an application*

Now to find the application delegate, we need to use [UIApplication sharedApplication].delegate, but since the variable a already refers to the instance of the app, we can access it via a.delegate. See Figure 4-18.

■ **Note**   Application delegate protocol defines methods that are called by a UIApplication object in response to important events in the app's lifetime.

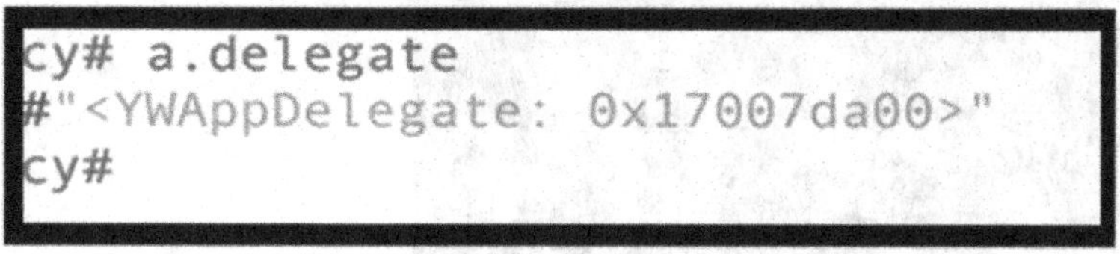

```
cy# a.delegate
#"<YWAppDelegate: 0x17007da00>"
cy#
```

Figure 4-18. *Application delegate*

So now we can play with the application runtime and modify its contents. The Yahoo! Weather app hides its status bar by default, but you can toggle the status bar using the same Objective-C code. See Figure 4-19.

```
[cy#
[cy# [a setStatusBarHidden:NO animated:NO]
 cy#
```

Figure 4-19. Using Cycript to manipulate application behavior

Notice in Figure 4-20 that the status bar is now visible. Let's look at another example where we change the notification badge count on the icon of the app.

Figure 4-20. Changing the status bar

And as you can see in Figures 4-21 and 4-22, the count of the notification badge of the app's icon on the home screen has changed to 100. This way you can tinker with a lot of app properties and define how the app will work during runtime.

```
[cy# [UIApplication sharedApplication].applicationIconBadgeNumber = 100;
100
cy#
```

Figure 4-21. *Altering the application icon badge using Cycript*

By now, you should be familiar with Cycript's capabilities. Cycript provides a whole new perspective of security testing of iOS apps during runtime. A few hints may be finding the login methods and directly calling the login success method from Cycript and try to bypass user logins or maybe changing app data.

Figure 4-22. *Application icon badge number changed*

Now lets see what else we can do using runtime manipulation. This time, we will do some runtime manipulation on the DVIA app (see Figure 4-23).

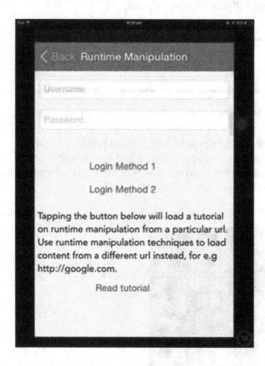

Figure 4-23. *Runtime manipulation in DVIA*

We will follow the same steps to hook the Cycript interpreter into the DVIA app's runtime and start analyzing the app (see Figure 4-24).

```
[Kunals-iPad-mini:~ root# cycript -p 786
cy# UIApp
#"<UIApplication: 0x147e127b0>"
cy# UIApp.delegate
#"<AppDelegate: 0x170054a00>"
```

Figure 4-24. *DVIA Cycript*

Let's run class-dump to dump all the Objective-C runtime information (class declarations and such) that's stored in the app binary. We learned to install class-dump in the previous chapter; you can install it on your iOS Device or your Mac.

This application has three runtime manipulation challenges. Two of them are login bypass and the third one is to change the URL of the tutorial that loads the blog URL. So we will change the URL from which the application will fetch the content and render in the web view.

If you click on Read Tutorial button, the screen that appears looks like Figure 4-25.

Figure 4-25. *Read tutorial normal screen*

Let's analyze the binary by dumping it using `class-dump`. For this example, we will be using `class-dump` on my Mac, as I already have the binary of the DVIA app on my machine. You can grab it from the IPA or drag it from the device using any SFTP client. See Figure 4-26.

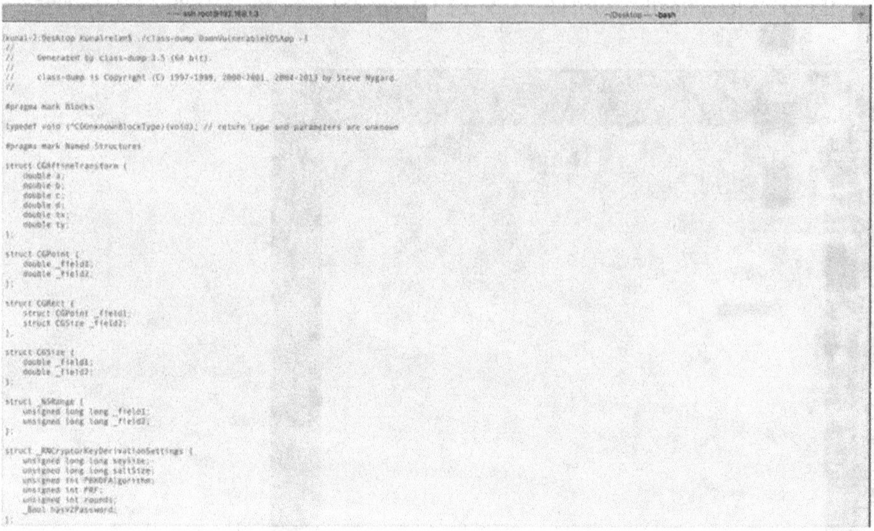

Figure 4-26. *Class-dump DVIA*

Now that we have the dump in our terminal, let's search for the URL variable that we need to edit to change the URL from which the app loads the tutorial content. It's shown in Figure 4-27.

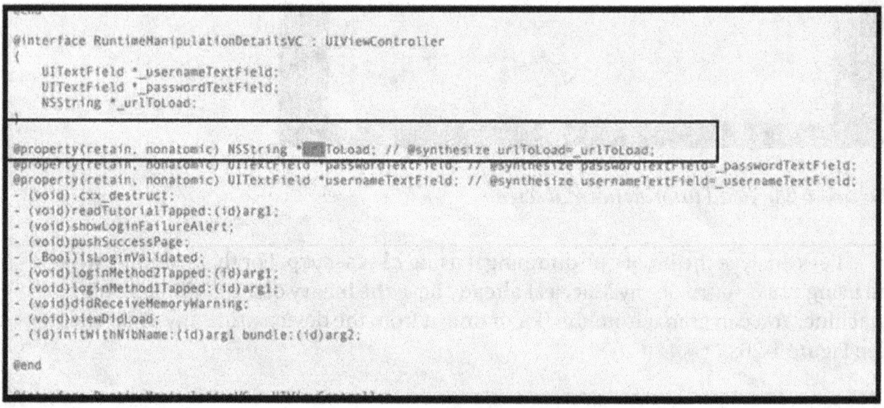

```
@interface RuntimeManipulationDetailsVC : UIViewController
{
    UITextField *_usernameTextField;
    UITextField *_passwordTextField;
    NSString *_urlToLoad;
}

@property(retain, nonatomic) NSString *   ToLoad; // @synthesize urlToLoad=_urlToLoad;
@property(retain, nonatomic) UITextField *passwordTextField; // @synthesize passwordTextField=_passwordTextField;
@property(retain, nonatomic) UITextField *usernameTextField; // @synthesize usernameTextField=_usernameTextField;
- (void).cxx_destruct;
- (void)readTutorialTapped:(id)arg1;
- (void)showLoginFailureAlert;
- (void)pushSuccessPage;
- (_Bool)isLoginValidated;
- (void)loginMethod2Tapped:(id)arg1;
- (void)loginMethod1Tapped:(id)arg1;
- (void)didReceiveMemoryWarning;
- (void)viewDidLoad;
- (id)initWithNibName:(id)arg1 bundle:(id)arg2;

@end
```

Figure 4-27. *Finding UrlToLoad*

While searching for the keyword url in the huge class dump, we found one instance that seems to be a good place to start. But if you look closely, it seems to be accurate as the view controller's class name is RuntimeManipulationDetailsVC and it has two variables that take a value from the text field—usernameTextField and passwordTextFieldwhich. We can see them in the Runtime Manipulation view of the DVIA app. So let's now open Cycript and change the value of the variable on runtime and load some other URL instead of the blog.

To change the value of the NSString type variable urlToLoad, you need to run the command shown in Figure 4-28.

```
icy#
[cy# RuntimeManipulationDetailsVC.messages['urlToLoad'] = function() { return "http://pentestninja.me";};
function () {return"http://pentestninja.me";}
cy#
```

Figure 4-28. *Changing the URL string*

Now that we have changed the URL, tapping the Read Tutorial button will load the HTML page of the www.pentestninja.me web site, as shown in Figure 4-29. This completes the URL challenge.

Figure 4-29. *Changed URL*

Similarly, we can also bypass the login view by tinkering with another method in the same view controller. If you notice in Figure 4-24 in the list of methods of the classRuntimeManipulationDetailsVC, there is a method called isLoginValidated that looks interesting. It returns a Boolean value to possibly decide whether the user is logged in. Let's try to change the function definition so that it always return YES (returning true to pass the function logic) and possibly bypass the login.

If you currently try to type a username/password combination, the app will show an alert saying that your guess is incorrect, obviously (see Figure 4-30). Hence, let's go back to the Cycript interpreter modify the function.

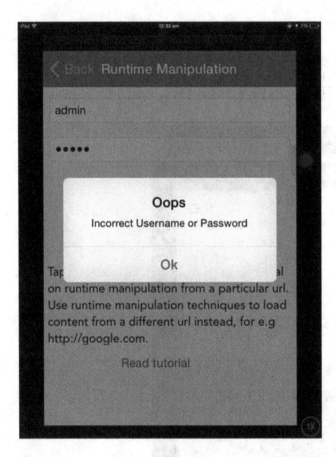

Figure 4-30. *DVIA login is denied*

Hook up your Cycript interpreter again. We are using the same view controller and changing the return type of the method isLoginValidated, which is pretty easy and straightforward (see Figure 4-31).

```
[cy# RuntimeManipulationDetailsVC.messages['isLoginValidated'] = function() { return YES;};
function () {return YES;}
cy#
```

Figure 4-31. *Changing the isLoginValidated method*

That's it. We have modified the function. This time if we tap on the login button with any username/password combination, the login bypassed view will be visible and that should confirm our success (see Figure 4-32).

Figure 4-32. *Login bypass view*

Summary

This chapter was all about using the tools we set up in last chapter, thus making your Cycript concepts stronger. The two applications used in this chapter to depict the vulnerability and using Cycript to execute runtime analysis and manipulation on application behavior.

In the coming chapter, we discuss iOS penetration testing and reverse engineering more in depth.

CHAPTER 5

■ ■ ■

iOS Security Toolkit

So far we have been digging deep into iOS application security and have covered the basic hacks to look for when testing iOS applications. In this chapter, we cover advanced and low-level iOS app security concepts that will give you an even better understanding and better skills for iOS app security testing. This chapter discusses disassembly iOS application binaries, advance runtime manipulation, and static analysis on iOS applications.

Advance Reverse Engineering

In last chapter, we bypassed the login screen with a runtime manipulation using Cycript. As you might have guessed, the login bypass was temporary and valid only for the particular instance of the application's execution, because all the changes are done in the memory (RAM) and upon restart they would have all been lost. What if you need a better solution where your changes become permanent and the application behaves this way every time it runs (i.e., it bypasses the login forever)? You can bypass the DVIA login so that it always logs in when you tap the login button.

To achieve this goal, you have to patch the DVIA app's binary and, for that, you use a disassembler that will translate the mach-O binary into assembly language. There are a couple of good disassemblers and debuggers in the market, including IDA-Pro, Hopper, etc. IDA Pro is a Windows, Linux, and OS X hosted multi-processor disassembler and debugger and is one the best available. Hopper is quite new but a really good disassembler for OS X and Linux and can disassemble iOS, Mac, Linux, and Windows executables like a charm. Hopper can disassemble any kind of binary, but its main platform is Objective-C and that's where it is really good. Therefore we will be using Hopper for our work.

Hopper is a commercial tool and costs around $100, but you can try a free evaluation copy with some limitations (time-limited sessions for half an hour). You can download the free version of Hopper from https://www.hopperapp.com/ and install it on your preferred operating system. I used my Mac (running OS X 10.11) for this example. We'll also use a bit of Assembly language for this task and we try to explain important terms and concepts. If you are new to ARM assembly programming (http://www.toves.org/books/arm/), I suggest you get a small primer on it, as covering it in detail is beyond the scope of this book.

© Kunal Relan 2016
K. Relan, *iOS Penetration Testing*, DOI 10.1007/978-1-4842-2355-0_5

At the time of writing this book, the login screen of the DVIA app looked something like what's shown in Figure 5-1. As you know from the previous chapter, the app throws an "incorrect username or password" error message when you try to log in with an invalid username or password.

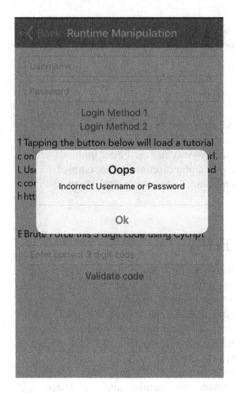

Figure 5-1. *DVIA login when you enter incorrect username or password*

Now you'll learn how to bypass this login screen permanently, using a disassembler. For that we have to fetch the binary from the directory of the installed app, from the device, and open it in the disassembler.

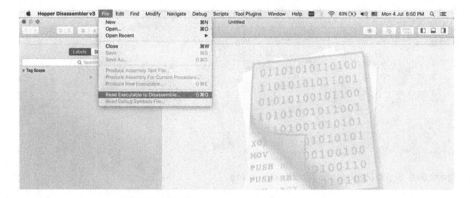

Figure 5-2. *Reading an executable to disassemble*

Once you open Hopper, choose Read Executable to Disassemble from the File menu and then find your executable on the disk (see Figure 5-2). It should have the name DamnVulnerableIOSApp, as shown in Figure 5-3.

Figure 5-3. *Finding the executable to disassemble*

After you select your executable, a popup menu opens. Leave all the settings to their defaults and click on OK to begin disassembling, as shown in Figure 5-4.

Figure 5-4. *Selecting defaults for disassembling*

Within a few seconds, the disassembler should have completed its disassembling process and you can start working on the disassembled binary. As you know from the previous chapter the view controller classname (`RuntimeManipulationDetailsVC`), you can straight away search for it. You know that the method was `loginMethod1Tapped`, as shown in Figure 5-5.

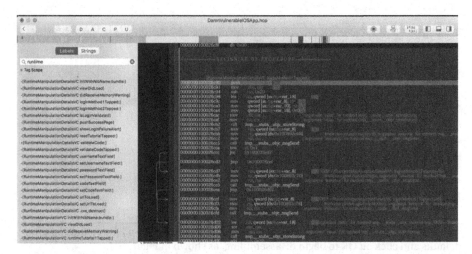

Figure 5-5. *The RuntimeManipulationDetailsVC page*

If you click on the `loginMethod1Tapped` method, you'll see the jump to memory address condition `jne0x100026cd7`, which redirects the instruction pointer to two different memory addresses, depending on the truth (blue arrow) or falsity (red arrow) of the jump condition. This relates to the correctness of the user input. If you check out the Control Flow Graph (CFG) by clicking on the CFG button on top-right corner, shown in Figure 5-6, you will see a flow chart of the method. Then, after checking out the different address, the method's jump to address `0x100026cd7` seems to be the one taking you to the login success screen. You can verify this by opening the disassembled page again and verifying that the memory address `0x10026cd7` shows the `pushSuccessPage` method name. You can also check out the pseudo-code of the flow by clicking on the pseudo-code button on top right. This will give you a better overview of the program structure and explain how you might bypass the login. Figure 5-6 shows the Control Flow Graph button and Figure 5-7 shows the graph.

***Figure 5-6.** Control Flow Graph button tab*

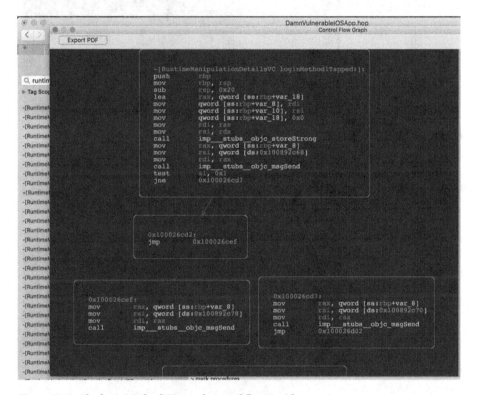

***Figure 5-7.** The loginMethod1Tapped control flow graph*

It might now be clear that we need to somehow make this method forcefully jump to the address 0x100026cd7, irrespective of the validity of the credentials, every time it is called. Let's see how we can manipulate the binary so that our theory works.

To start with, click on the last statement of the method and then go to Modify ➤ Assemble Instruction so that you can change the last instruction to jump to the address of the pushSuccessPage method.

Once you choose Assemble Instruction, as shown in Figure 5-8, a window will pop up, as shown in Figure 5-9. From there, you enter the instruction you are modifying.

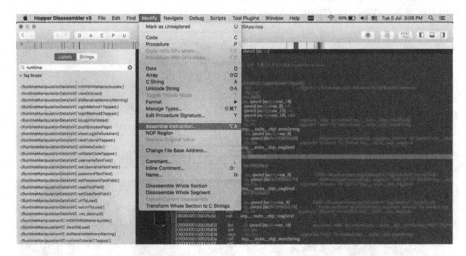

Figure 5-8. *Assemble instruction*

To change the instruction to jump to 0x100026cd7, type the instruction in Assembly language syntax, i.e., jmp 0x100026cd7. Then click on the Assemble and Go Next button (see Figure 5-9).

Figure 5-9. *Changing instruction*

You've changed the instruction, so it's time to save a new executable code and see if it really worked.

Select File ➤ Produce New Executable and replace the new executable with the one in your app directory.

Once you have replaced the executable, you need to kill all the running instances of the app from the memory and then restart the app.

When you open your DVIA, go to the Runtime Manipulation module and tap on the Login Method 1. This time, a success page opens, as shown in Figure 5-10. It confirms that you successfully bypassed the user login persistently.

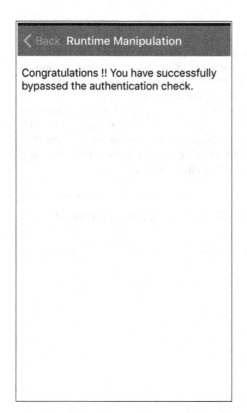

Figure 5-10. *User login bypass*

A Day in the Life of a Debugger

Debugging is a very important part of software development. Code doesn't always do what we expect it to do. In such cases, the debugger is our friend and helps us figure out the things going wrong and saves time. However, the debugger can also be used as a tool to understand someone else's code or even your own code, without documentation or comments. Apple has very mature debuggers on its platform. LLDB Debugger replaced GDB in Xcode 5, becoming the primary debugging tool in iOS and OS X development. LLDB is an advanced debugger and can easily be mapped to work like GDB.

If you are an iOS or OS X developer, you might already be familiar with both of these tools. The site http://lldb.llvm.org/lldb-gdb.html has a very good explanation of GDB to LLDB mapping. LLDB has a command-line interface, but Apple has a relatively approachable GUI for LLDB. Debugging is a very vast topic and there are tons of books and other resources available in the market on debugging. However, this section introduces some of the basic yet important concept of iOS app debugging.

Debugging in Xcode

Xcode has useful tools for debugging and the graphical UI version of those debugging tools take it to next level by making it very easy to get familiar with it in a relatively short period. However, you can use them from their command-line interfaces as well. We will discuss LLDB followed by an introduction to debugging with Xcode.

LLDB's GUI interface makes it quite easy to understand and use. Setting a breakpoint is as easy as clicking next to the method you want to set the breakpoint on (see Figure 5-11). A *breakpoint* is a signal that tells the debugger to pause the execution of the program at a particular point. it allows you to trigger some command or change values of variables at runtime, and breakpoints can be easily resumed from the same state.

■ **Note**   A *breakpoint* is a point in a program that, when reached, triggers a special behavior for debugging purposes.

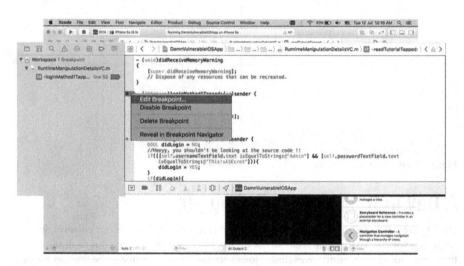

Figure 5-11. Setting a breakpoint

For example in Figure 5-11, you can see that setting a breakpoint is as simple as clicking on the left panel of a statement. You can check out the list of all your breakpoints in different files in the left panel of the Breakpoints tab, as shown in Figure 5-12.

Figure 5-12. *The Breakpoints tab*

The Breakpoints tab is highlighted in Figure 5-12 in the black square for your better understanding. Once the code hits the breakpoint, the LLDB is triggered and the program execution is paused. You will see the LLDB shell in your output console when it's on a breakpoint, because that is the place where you execute all your debugging commands. See Figure 5-13.

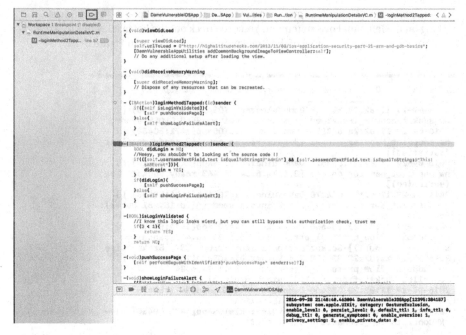

Figure 5-13. *LLDB triggering*

In the panel in Figure 5-13, we set a breakpoint on the `loginMethod1Tapped` method in the `RuntimeManipulationDetailsVC.m` file. We can also edit the breakpoint or reveal the breakpoint from this menu, which pops up upon clicking the breakpoint.

Here are some ways you can set breakpoints from command line

```
(lldb) breakpoint set --name functionOne --name functionTwo
(lldb) breakpoint set --selector someSelector:
(lldb) breakpoint set --method myOwnMethod
(lldb) breakpoint set --name "-[myOwnVCmyOwnMethod:]"
```

LLDB and GDB both do a shortest unique string match on command names, hence, short forms of commands also work.

```
(lldb) b set --name functionOne
```

Figure 5-14. *Calling a breakpoint*

Once you run the application after setting the breakpoint, everything works the same way. However as soon as execution reaches the method with the breakpoint, you will see some changes in your console and will get the current address of your execution (see Figure 5-14). You can also study the upcoming statements of the program from the current (breakpoint hit) line. If you analyze this you can have a clear understanding of the program's behavior. See Figure 5-15.

Figure 5-15. *Analyzing program execution using breakpoints*

You can check out all your current breakpoints by typing this command into the console:

```
(lldb) break list
```

You'll get a list similar to the one shown in Figure 5-16.

```
) Thread 1 ) 🕭 0 -[RuntimeManipulationDetailsVC loginMethod1Tapped:]

2016-07-12 01:13:04.351
DamnVulnerableIOSApp[27530:7188028] Flurry: Starting
session on Agent Version [Flurry_iOS_151_6.4.0]
(lldb) break list
Current breakpoints:
1: file = '/Users/kunalrelan/Documents/Developer/ios/DVIA-
master/DVIA/DamnVulnerableIOSApp/DamnVulnerableIOSApp/
RuntimeManipulationDetailsVC.m', line = 55, exact_match =
0, locations = 1, resolved = 1, hit count = 1

  1.1: where = DamnVulnerableIOSApp`-
[RuntimeManipulationDetailsVC loginMethod1Tapped:] + 39 at
RuntimeManipulationDetailsVC.m:56, address =
0x0000000104650cb7, resolved, hit count = 1

(lldb)
```

Figure 5-16. *Getting breakpoints*

The LLDB command gives you detailed information about your breakpoints. You can also set more breakpoints from this console using this method. If you want to set many breakpoints at the same time, you can use a regular expression to match a particular string and set breakpoints in groups.

```
Thread 1 〉 [icon] 0 -[RuntimeManipulationDetailsVC loginMethod1Tapped:]

2016-07-12 01:20:54.678
DamnVulnerableIOSApp[27690:7194048] Flurry: Starting
session on Agent Version [Flurry_iOS_151_6.4.0]
(lldb) break set -r login
Breakpoint 2: 45 locations.
(lldb) |
```

Figure 5-17. *Setting breakpoints with RegEx*

As you can see in Figure 5-17, with this simple RegEx command, you could set 45 breakpoints in the app that match the string "login".

You can disable a breakpoint at any time with this command:

"(lldb) breakpoint disable"

So now imagine all the interesting things you can do with breakpoints, such as bypassing app flows in runtime, changing values of variables in runtime, modifying resources, etc., just by halting the program execution at any desired location.

Debugging using LLDB can be crucial and important at the same time; the way you use this tool is really important. LLDB debugger's features and its capabilities is a big topic in itself and you need to have coding experience or at least understand it to master the art of debugging. Let's check out some things you can and will do with LLDB.

You can also check a variable's current value using the LLDB debugger, which can help you analyze and do a lot of work when it comes to penetration testing. Just like we did in runtime manipulation, we can see the current URL of the blog in the variable called urlToLoad. See Figure 5-18.

Figure 5-18. *Reading variables using LLDB*

LLDB can also help you automate a lot of options when debugging applications, like filling out forms and submitting them automatically. This can save a lot of time. You can easily do this using the Add Action button from the Edit breakpoint menu, which allows you to add expressions that will be evaluated when a particular breakpoint gets hit. See Figure 5-19.

Let's find out how we can change the value of the variable urlToLoad during runtime using LLDB.

Figure 5-19. *The Add Action button in LLDB*

If you see `viewDidLoad`, it assigns a value to the variable `urlToLoad` and thus we will set a breakpoint at the end of the function, after it has assigned a value to the variable we want to tinker with. After that, when we click on our breakpoint, it should show a dialog into which we can add an action.

Clicking on the Add Action button will add a text field to this popup, where we can put our command that we want to evaluate. See Figure 5-20.

```
expr self.urlToLoad = @"http://pentestninja.me"
```

Figure 5-20. *Changing the urlToLoad value*

You need to prepend the keyword `expr` to tell the debugger that the action is an expression followed by the actual expression you want to execute. Here, we just change the value of the variable `urlToLoad` to a different URL. Similarly, multiple variables can be assigned values as well, which can be useful to automate form submissions during the debug phase. You should also choose the Automatically Continue After Evaluating Actions option, which will continue the execution after evaluating the action expression.

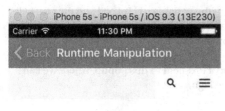

Figure 5-21. Changed urlToLoad variable

You are finally able to load your own URL in the application by tweaking the urlToLoad variable. See Figure 5-21.

As you can see, it was really easy to change the value of urlToLoad at runtime, and these types of utilities come in handy when you're doing debugging and checking how an app actually works.

We'll now discuss debugging third-party apps and seeing what things can be done using LLDB.

Debugging third-party apps is also quite easy with LLDB; however, we have to set up the whole environment. This includes setting up debugserver, which is an Apple utility used by Xcode to debug applications on a device. debugserver is installed automatically in the device once you start testing an app; however, it can only debug applications that are signed by the particular provisioning profile that contains the signing identities of your application, because lack of entitlement to allow task_for_pid() helps you get the task port of a process. To debug all the applications, you'll create a new entitlement profile which will have this flag set to True by default.

The debugserver is currently stored in a read-only RAM disk in OS X (macOS), so you need to copy the application to a directory having write privileges and then use that debugserver for debugging.

Let's now set up debugserver and start debugging third-party apps on our jailbroken device.

The first step to this is to mount the Xcode's developer disk image and copy the debugserver to the desktop or to any other location with write privileges. See Figure 5-22.

The command for this would be as follows, which we need to run on the Terminal:

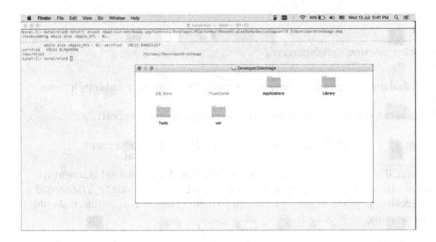

Figure 5-22. *Mounting the developer disk image*

```
$ hdiutil attach /Applications/Xcode.app/Contents/Developer/Platforms/
iPhoneOS.platform/DeviceSupport/[Your iOS Version Here]/DeveloperDiskImage.
dmg
```

Once this is done, we need to create a file named entitlements.plist, which will enable the debugserver to run the unsigned code with following data in it.

```
<?xml version="1.0" encoding="UTF-8"?>
<!DOCTYPEplist PUBLIC "-//Apple//DTD PLIST 1.0//EN"   "http://www.apple.com/
DTDs/ PropertyList-1.0.dtd">

<key>com.apple.springboard.debugapplications
<true/>
<key>run-unsigned-code
<true/>
<key>get-task-allow
<true/>
<key>task_for_pid-allow
```

```
<true/>
```

You can also download this from https://gist.github.com/kunal-relan/2acdf1f bb52c3f781e77093238618521.

We will then re-sign the debugserver to the newly created entitlements.plist file so that the debugserver can debug all the third-party apps.

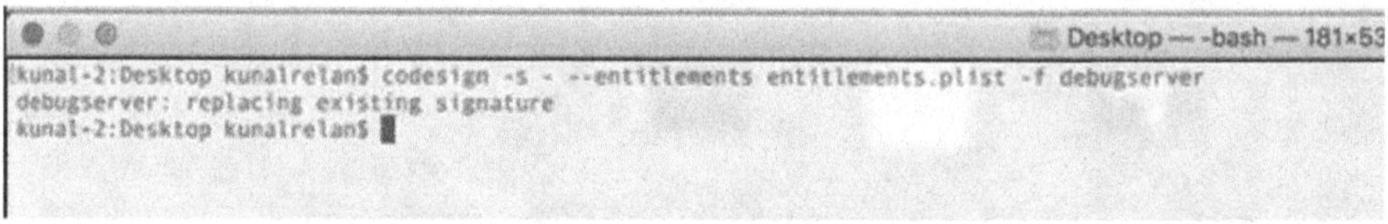

Figure 5-23. *Code signing debugserver*

You'll find the debugserver binary inside the usr/bin directory and copy it to our desktop.

Now you can run the following command to re-sign the debugserver:

```
$ codesign -s - --entitlements entitlements.plist -f debugserver
```

However, if you are using a 64-bit device you may need to use the entitlements. plist file available at https://gist.github.com/kunal-relan/0eaa2e1ee37505ea9ad ac83f044edebb or copy the following code into your entitlements.plist file. It should then work properly.

```
<?xml version="1.0" encoding="UTF-8"?>
<!DOCTYPEplist PUBLIC "-//Apple//DTD PLIST 1.0//EN" "http://www.apple.com/
DTDs/ PropertyList-1.0.dtd">
<plist version="1.0">
<dict>
<key>com.apple.springboard.debugapplications</key>
<true/>
<key>run-unsigned-code</key>
<true/>
<key>get-task-allow</key>
<true/>
<key>task_for_pid-allow</key>
<true/>
```

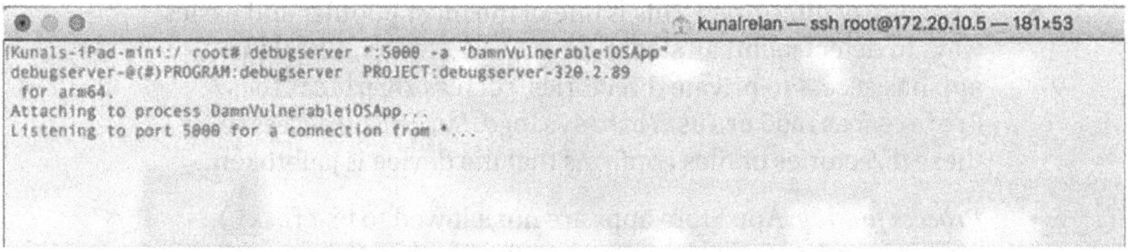

Figure 5-24. *Starting debugserver*

```
</dict>
</plist>
```

After completing all the steps, you need to copy this debugserver binary to your device using SCP. You'll then be good to go and start debugging third-party iOS apps. Now we will start the debugserver on our device, as shown in Figure 5-24, and start debugging the apps.

Since the debugserver is now listening on port 5000, we will connect our OS X terminal to the device on port 5000. On the terminal, you start lldb by typing lldb and then connect to the device.

```
$ lldb
```

This should start the lldb allowing you to further connect to the device.

Bypassing Jailbreak Detection

Many App Store apps have started implementing procedures to check the authenticity of the device on which the app is being installed. Every app developer may not have the exact same way of detecting jailbreak status. There are quite a few ways to detect the jailbreak status of a device. Most of the time, app developers do jailbreak detection to disable functionalities of the application, to be on the safe side, as they are worried about their customers' private data. Jailbreak detection has many pathways, but all of them can be bypassed by one or another trick.

Apps generally use one or a combination of the following techniques to check the jailbreak status of a device:

- *Directory permissions*: This method works by checking the UNIX file permissions of certain files and directories using NSFileManager APIs and/or lower-level C functions like statfs(), as jailbroken devices allow full file-system permissions and jailed devices do not.

- *Existence of directories*: This is one of the most popular and easies ways to detect jailbreak status. It works by determining if the app has access to private directories, such as /Applications/ Preferences.app or /usr/bin/syslogd. Successful access to these directories or files confirms that the device is jailbroken.

- *Process forking*: App Store apps are not allowed to use fork(), popen(), and so on, or any other similar low-level system calls for child process creation in a jailed device. However, on a jailbroken device, these calls are executed successfully. By checking the returned pid(Process ID) from a fork() call, apps can detect the jailbroken status of the device.

■ **Note**   fork() is a system call that creates processes in UNIX/Linux, whereas popen() is used to initiate pipe streams to or from a process.

- *system()*: Calling the system() function on a jailed device returns 0 but on a jailbroken device it returns 1, which is a straightforward jailbreak detection.

- *Loopback SSH connection*: This one is not really accurate but works on the assumption that every jailbroken device has OpenSSH installed on it and tries connecting to the SSH server on the device's via its home address (127.0.0.1). Most of the time, users leave the default SSH password unchanged (for the root user, it's alpine). This makes it easier to detect.

- *dyld functions*: This is the hardest to get around, and it works by calling functions like _dyld_image_count() and _dyld_get_ image_name() to see which dylibs are loaded.

```
@end

@interface JailbreakDetectionVC : UIViewController
{
}

- (_Bool)isJailbroken;
- (void)jailbreakTest2Tapped:(id)arg1;
- (void)jailbreakTest1Tapped:(id)arg1;
- (void)readArticleTapped:(id)arg1;
- (void)didReceiveMemoryWarning;
- (void)viewDidLoad;
- (id)initWithNibName:(id)arg1 bundle:(id)arg2;

@end

@interface RNOpenSSLDecryptor : RNDecryptor
{
    NSString *_password;
    struct _RNCryptorSettings _settings;
}

+ (id)decryptData:(id)arg1 withEncryptionKey:(id)arg2 HMACKey:(id)arg3 error:(id *)arg4;
+ (id)decryptData:(id)arg1 withPassword:(id)arg2 error:(id *)arg3;
+ (id)decryptData:(id)arg1 withSettings:(struct _RNCryptorSettings)arg2 encryptionKey:(id)arg3 IV:(id)arg4 error:(id *)arg5;
+ (id)decryptData:(id)arg1 withSettings:(struct _RNCryptorSettings)arg2 password:(id)arg3 error:(id *)arg4;
@property(nonatomic) struct _RNCryptorSettings settings; // @synthesize settings=_settings;
@property(copy, nonatomic) NSString *password; // @synthesize password=_password;

            jailbreak                                                    Find
```

Figure 5-25. *DVIA class dump*

Let's hit the DVIA app again and bypass the jailbreak detection mechanism. First, let's class dump the binary. If you don't have it by now, use the same methods we discussed in the earlier chapter to get it.

DVIA uses two methods for jailbreak detection. Let's start with the first one and search for the keyword Jailbreak, which will probably give us what we are looking for. See Figure 5-25.

```
module      5590   0.0   0.4   340000   4112   ??   SS   2.40PM   0.00.07 /usr/libexec/
Kunals-iPad-mini:~ root# cycript -p 8299
cy# UIApp
#"<UIApplication: 0x154e12590>"
```

Figure 5-26. *Hooking DVIA*

If you look closely at Figure 5-25, you can see the view controller named JailbreakDetectionVC. Inside it, there is a method called isJailbroken that has a Boolean type return value. So it let's fire up Cycript to try out our attempt at runtime and later you can make your hack permanent by disassembling and recompiling it.

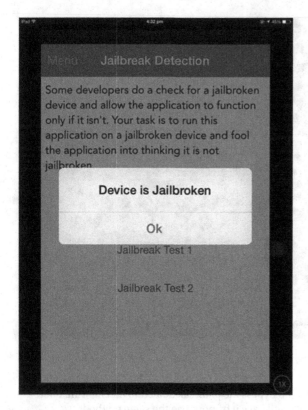

Figure 5-27. *Device jailbreak status*

Fire up DVIA in the device and hook it using Cycript (see Figure 5-26). Start inspecting it.

As you might be guessing, we need to make the isJailbroken method return a NO value (false) for our bypass to work and that is it. Currently in the app, if we tap on

```
[cy# JailbreakDetectionVC.messages["isJailbroken"] = function() {return NO;}
function () {return NO;}
cy# ▉
```

Figure 5-28. *Changing isJailbroken*

Jailbreak Test 1, it should show the message "Device is Jailbroken" (see Figure 5-27). However, with our runtime patching it won't show it anymore.

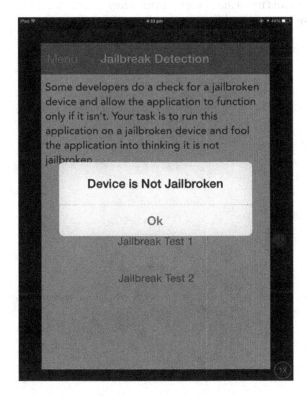

Figure 5-29. Jailbreak status bypassed

In the Cycript shell, you need to change the method's return value by typing the following statement (see Figure 5-28):

```
Cy# JailbreakDetectionVC.messages["isJailbroken"] = function() {return NO;}
```

And that is it. Now, if we tap on the Jailbreak Test 1 button again, we'll see a different message ("Device is Not Jailbroken" as shown in Figure 5-29). This means our bypass was successful.

So now the second jailbreak detection challenge doesn't get bypassed the same way, but you can attempt to solve it with the help of a debugger (LLDB) at runtime. I will leave that as an exercise for you. If you need help, check out the solution at https:// pentestninja.me.

Summary

This chapter discussed advanced reverse engineering, disassembling applications, and runtime manipulation. You should try all the examples in this chapter on DVIA. In Chapter 6, you'll learn see how to automate different parts of your iOS application penetration testing.

CHAPTER 6

■ ■ ■

Automating App Testing

So far we have learned about manual penetration testing and reverse engineering of an iOS app. In this chapter, we will check out various automated testing modules and toolsets for performing penetration testing on third-party apps. You will learn to use different open source tools in this chapter.

Automation has been a popular strategy for testers ever since repetitive tasks became an overhead issue after a certain point of time and people wanted to utilize resources in more complex areas that needed human attention. Manual testing is the most reliable method when it comes to testing an app's security, but many tools can provide handy assistance when time is a constraint.

In this chapter, we will work with IDB, which is a tool with a GUI and was built using Ruby. It can run many common and repetitive tasks like keychain dumping, plist extraction, etc., which you'll perform in every penetration test. This chapter also covers another tool called iRET (iOS Reverse Engineering Toolkit), which is designed to automate common tasks associated with iOS penetration testing. It automates tasks like reading the log and plist files, binary dumping, etc.

idb: Simplify Penetration Test

IDB is a tool written using Ruby for iOS. It automates a lot of tasks related to penetration testing and research, therefore saving a lot of time. IDB is a bit unstable on some devices as reported by some users; however, it works seamlessly on most the devices. Let's set up IDB and see how it can help.

You can check more about IDB at www.idbtool.com. As it's written using Ruby, you will obviously need Ruby installed on your machine and need to install RubyGems, which is a package manager for Ruby.

Apart from Ruby and RubyGems, other dependencies that need to be installed are qt, cmake, usbmuxd, and libimobiledevice. usbmuxd and libimobiledevice should be installed on your Mac if you have followed the previous chapters. However, you can install the rest of these using the Homebrew package manager on OS X. IDB can also be installed on Linux by following the installing instructions on its web site. We only cover OS X in this book.

Once you have all the prerequisites installed on your machine, the IDB tool can be installed using RubyGems simply by typing gem install idb in your Terminal. After installation, you can launch IDB by typing idb on your Terminal, as shown in Figure 6-1.

© Kunal Relan 2016
K. Relan, *iOS Penetration Testing*, DOI 10.1007/978-1-4842-2355-0_6

Figure 6-1. Launching IDB on OS X

Now you need to set up the SSH connection (IP, username, and password) to your iOS device so that IDB can connect to your device. For this, just go to Ruby (top-left in the menu bar) and select Preferences ➤ Device Config. Select Configure IDB to connect to your iOS device. Once you are done, click on Save and connect IDB to your device.

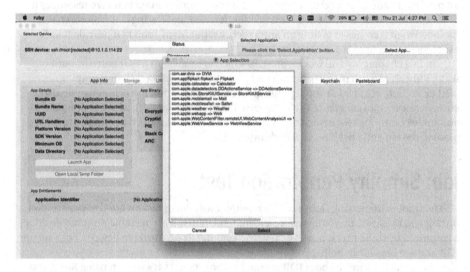

Figure 6-2. Configuring IDB

After connecting to your device, you can select the app you want to work on by clicking on the Select App button (as shown in Figure 6-3) and selecting your desired app from the list of apps shown in the popup dialog. Since we have already been working on DVIA, we will stick to the same for this chapter and start working with IDB.

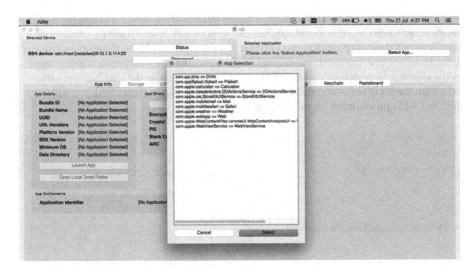

Figure 6-3. *Selecting an app to pen-test*

And after selecting the app, you can try using different tools in IDB to facilitate the penetration test (see Figure 6-4).

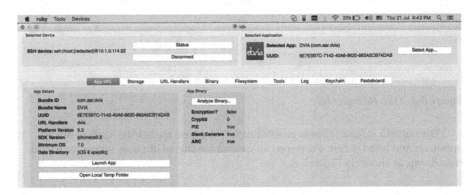

Figure 6-4. *DVIA pen-testing*

Once you have selected the DVIA app, notice that the nine tabs in the second row are activated. We will take a look at each one by one to understand their purpose. We start with the second one, the Storage tab. Clicking on this tab allows you to view the plist files, SQLite databases, and the cache database.

Let's start by checking out the plist files of this app. By now, you should be familiar with the plist files and the amount of data you can get from an application, which can help us in our penetration test.

So now you can look around for all the sensitive information the application might be revealing in different forms. Let's see the different ways we can use IDB to extract the same information from the application.

The next tab is called URL Handlers. It allows us not only to view the list of URL handlers registered by the selected app, but also to manually invoke them by arbitrary data to understand their purpose. You can also fuzz test the input validation done on each one of them. However, you can also fire up other URL handlers that are not specifically registered by the selected App, such as tel:// or http://. Once you click on the URL handler called dvia from the list of registered URLs and click Open (as shown in Figure 6-5), you will see that the DVIA app launches on your device.

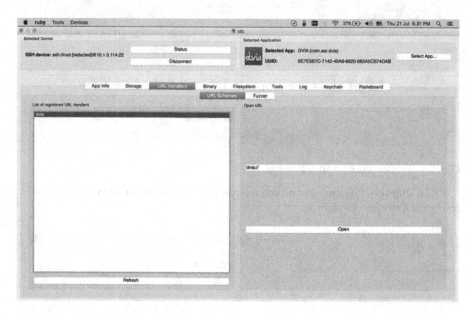

Figure 6-5. *URL Handlers tab*

The next tab is Binary, but to enable this tab, you have to click the Analyze Binary button on App Info tab first. Then you can view all the shared libraries, strings, and weak class dump, as shown in Figure 6-6.

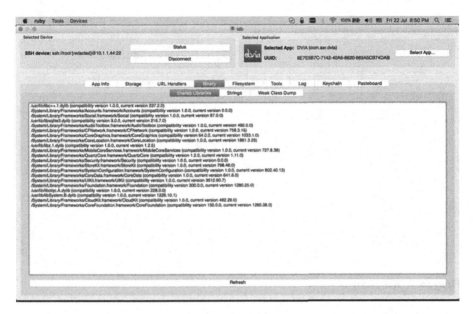

Figure 6-6. *Binary analyzing*

In the next tab, called Filesystem, you can check out the file system related information of the application and view the files contents in its directories.

The Tools tab allows you to view the screenshots taken by iOS when an app goes in the background. You can determine if these screenshots reveal any confidential data and use it as a way to find to insecure parts of the application. It also has a certificate manager for managing SSL certificates, which will help you intercept HTTPS traffic like we did with Charles Proxy. Finally, you can edit the device's host file, which allows you to map hostnames to IPs.

The next tab, called Log, is really interesting and is not scoped to this particular app. Rather it streams the device syslog, which can reveal a lot of insightful information. This utility also streams app data, logged using the NSLog API, which sometimes may reveal highly sensitive data. So you should always look out for it while pen-testing an app. See Figure 6-7.

101

Figure 6-7. iOS syslog

Next comes the Keychain dump, which is nothing but has the same uses as the keychain-dumping tool discussed in the previous chapter. This is the same manager of that tool integrated into IDB.

It's an amazing utility that gathers all keychain information from the device with a click. As you can see in Figure 6-8, it dumped the auth token of my Facebook login stored in my device's keychain.

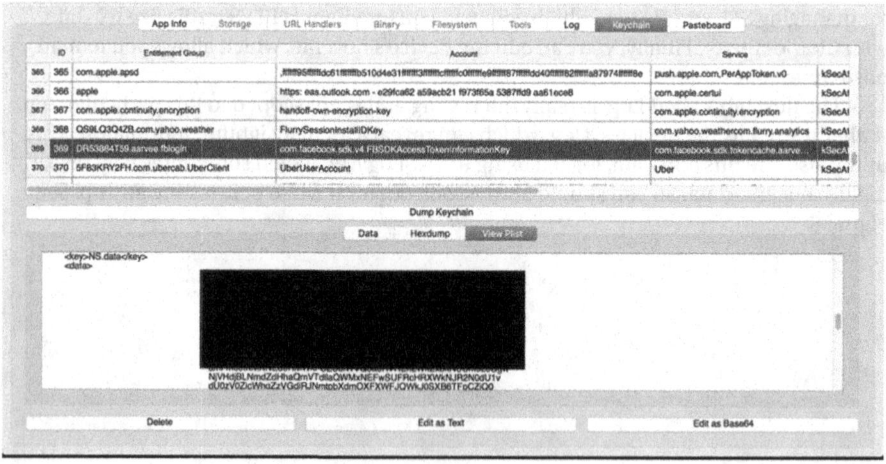

Figure 6-8. Keychain dumping

The last tab in IDB is Pasteboard. This tab reads the data stored on the device's pasteboard (also called the clipboard). Sometimes it contains a lot of private information. All you need to do, to view the Pasteboard contents in real time, is click the Start button. Whenever something is copied to the device, it can be fetched in real time and stored in the logs. See Figure 6-9.

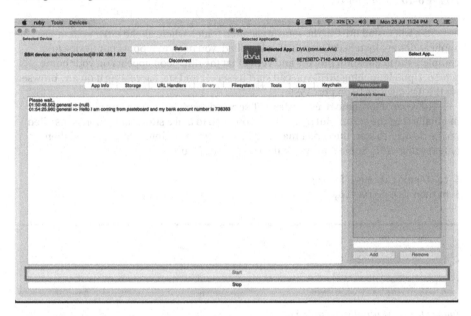

Figure 6-9. *Pasteboard capturing*

So that was all about IDB. Surely this tool will be an important part of your iOS penetration-testing arsenal. Its ease of use is a huge benefit to speed up your penetration-test process. In the next section, we discuss iRET and its utilization.

iRET: iOS Reverse Engineering Toolkit

iOS Reverse Engineering Toolkit (iRET) is a toolkit designed to automate a lot of the common tasks executed while performing a penetration test and during the reverse engineering of the application. It automates repetitive actions with a click and hence is useful especially when performing penetration tests as a routine. It is very similar to IDB but has different tools that help us achieve different tasks. Installing iRET on the iOS device is also pretty easy; all you need to do is get the Debian package from https://github.com/S3Jensen/iRET and then install the binary using the same Debian package installer command ipkg. See Figure 6-10.

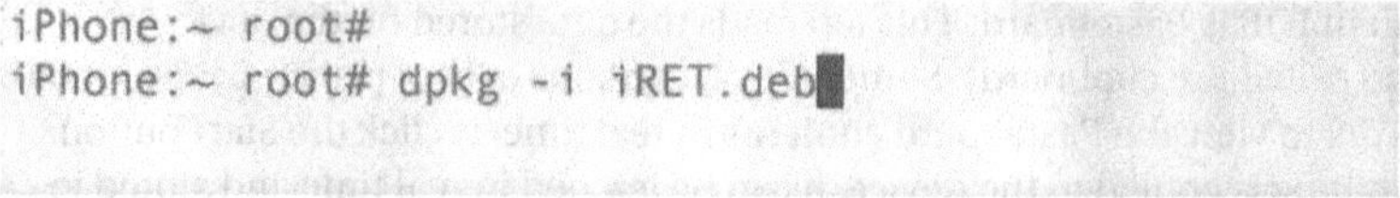

```
iPhone:~ root#
iPhone:~ root# dpkg -i iRET.deb
```

Figure 6-10. Installing iRET

This will install iRET in the root application folder, where all the other system applications are installed. Once iRET is installed, you need to reboot your device to complete the installation process and verify that the iRET icon appears on your home screen. Upon launching iRET, you can start its server and start accessing it on any browser via the iOS device's IP on port 5555.

However, if for some reason, the iRET server doesn't boot up by the app, you can manually start the server. But before that, you need to make sure that Python is installed on the device. To start the server manually, go to /Applications/iRE.app/ and then enter python iRE_Server.py to run the server. (See Figure 6-11.)

```
$ cd /Applications/iRE.app
$ python Ire_Server.py
```

Figure 6-11. Manually triggering iRET

Now the server will start running on port 5555, which we can access on the device's IP address.

As you can see in Figure 6-12, iRET is listening on 192.168.1.5:5555. Let's check out the web interface of iRET and explore all the available features .

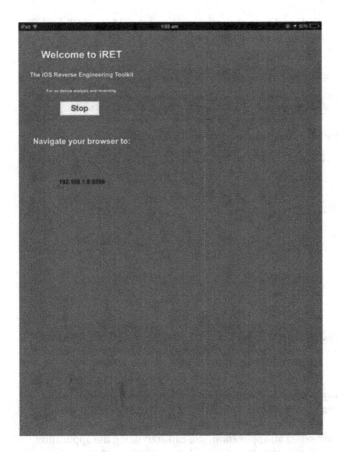

Figure 6-12. The iRET home screen

iRET expects you to have some tools installed on your device. Before proceeding, ensure you have these tools available or use these links to install them:

- oTool (http://www.unix.com/man-page/osx/1/otool/)

- dumpDecrypted (https://github.com/stefanesser/ dumpdecrypted)

- SQLite

- Theos (http://iphonedevwiki.net/index.php/Theos/Setup)

- Keychain_dumper (https://github.com/ptoomey3/Keychain-Dumper)

- File

- Plutil (http://ericasadun.com/ftp/EricaUtilities/)

- Class-dump-z (iOS version of class-dump)

Once you set up all the tools and open the web portal, you should see iRET with all the green highlights, indicating you are good to go. See Figure 6-13.

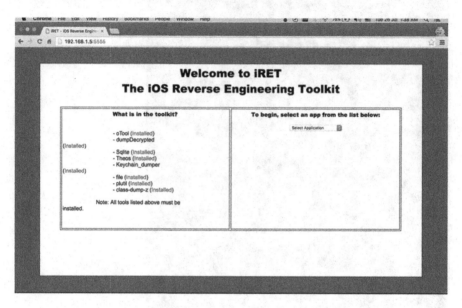

Figure 6-13. *The iRET web panel*

Now that you are ready to use iRET, you need to select the target application and begin the penetration-testing process of the app. As always, we will again choose our favorite DVIA app as the target.

Once you load iRET and select an application, you can start doing the application analysis using the utilities iRET provides. When you select an app from the home page, iRET starts analyzing and redirects you to the Binary Analysis Results tab, as shown in Figure 6-14.

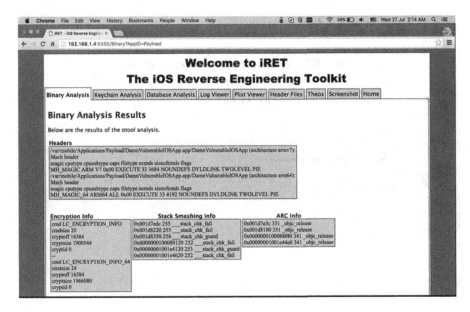

Figure 6-14. Application analysis results

The first tab that opens (Binary Analysis Results) shows up the otool analysis of the application binary. Whenever you select the application from the home drop-down, otool analysis of the binary is done in the background. You can see the status of the binary right on your screen.

The next tab—Keychain Analysis—is quite important. It gives you access to the keychain data, which is supposed to a highly secured and confidential area of storage in iOS. Unfortunately after jailbreaking, all that confidentiality goes out the window with the Keychain_dumper utility. As you can see in Figure 6-15, keychain dumper shows the dumped DB of keychain in a better, more manageable way.

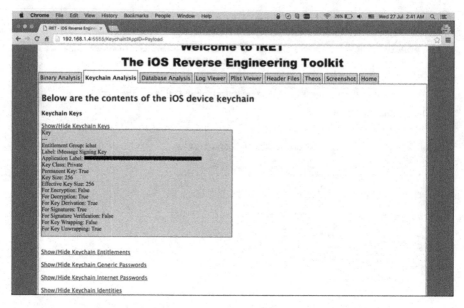

Figure 6-15. *The keychain dumper*

You can check out the whole keychain DB according to what you want to work on and want to check out, rather than getting the dump on your Terminal and trying to find the meaningful data from there. This makes it a really good utility for playing with the keychain data. The best part about this is that it separates the keychain data according to the type so you can view keys, entitlements, passwords, and identities separately.

Next in the row is Database Analysis tab. It's a pretty simple but useful tool that fetches the .db files from the Application data directory and makes them accessible over the portal in a very easy-to-browse manner. It uses the application's data directory and dumps all the .db files that show up here in the Database Analysis tab. You can then check out all the data inside those files. Many times as we have already seen, we get a lot of sensitive information that can be used for further exploitation.

This tool lays out the tables in the DB in a very proper manner and specifically dumps all the tables in the DB, as you can see in Figure 6-16.

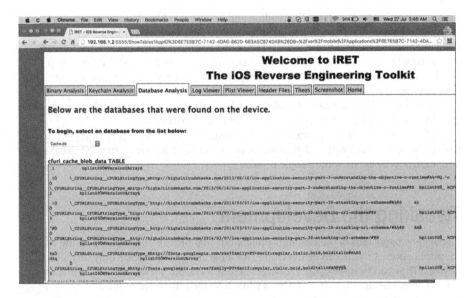

Figure 6-16. *Database analysis*

The next tab is Log Viewer and it has two functions compiled into a single tab; i.e., it has a syslog file viewer and an application log file viewer. If you see the top of it, you can toggle the link to see the first 100 lines of your system logs, which shows a lot of confidential information. Then it has another section that fetches the .txt and other text files in the application folder that might also turn out to be log files. See Figure 6-17.

Figure 6-17. *The log viewer*

In our case it just contains the readme and license text files, but in many cases I have seen there is a lot of confidential data in these files, such as API keys. So if you are a developer, you should take care to avoid such bad coding practices, as we have already discussed all the places where you should take extra precautions in storing your app-related confidential information. The client end is the worst place to store confidential data and every piece of information stored there should be extra secure.

So you saw all the content of README.txt here; similarly in the next tab, you can view the plist files and their contents stored in the application folder.

After checking out these two penetration-testing tools, let's jump to a different part of iOS application security—tweak development. In this section, you learn what tweaks are and learn how to create some simple tweaks.

Tweaking the Development

Tweaks are extensions of the existing applications that provide more utility on the top of the application. A tweak can be developed for a particular application only on jailbroken devices. They can be developed in many different ways, but we will try developing one using Theos. We already installed Theos while installing iRET. Theos is a widely used tool for tweak development and is, essentially, a suite of development tools that allows development and deploying of iOS apps, tweaks etc., without having to use Xcode. Theos comes as a self-contained package and can be installed on the desktop or on the iOS device. In this example, we will install it on our device and then code the tweak on our desktop.

You can learn more about Theos at http://iphonedevwiki.net/index.php/Theos. They have a tutorial for installing Theos on multiple platforms in case you are interested in installing it on your Linux or Windows machine. Once you have set up and installed Theos and its dependencies, which are Perl and iOS toolchain, you can set up the SDK for development. You can get a list of available SDKs at https://sdks.website/ and find the specific SDK in your development environment. As per the scope of this book, we will be installing it on our iOS device. See Figure 6-18.

```
kunalrelan — ssh root@10.1.0.36 — 181×53
[Kunals-iPad-mini:~ root# mkdir $THEOS/sdks
```

Figure 6-18. *Setting up the SDK*

You then get your specific SDK in that folder using curl. If you have yet not installed curl, go to Cydia and install curl on the device. For now, we will install SDK 9.3 on the iOS device, as shown in Figure 6-19.

```
[Kunals-iPad-mini:~ root# curl -ksL "https://sdks.website/dl/iPhoneOS9.3.sdk.tbz2" | tar -xj -C $THEOS/sdks
```

Figure 6-19. *Installing SDK 9.3*

Once you have installed the SDK, you can proceed with further configuring to start with tweak development.

You can set up your environment variables for Theos using this bash command.

```
$ export THEOS = /opt/theos
If you are running a 64-bit device, and you should run the given commands
for supporting these 64-bit devices.
n -s $THEOS/makefiles/platform/Darwin-arm.mk $THEOS/makefiles/platform/
Darwin-arm64.mk
ln -s $THEOS/makefiles/targets/Darwin-arm $THEOS/makefiles/targets/
Darwin-arm64
```

And once you have set up Theos, you may need to dump the device's private headers or get someone else's device headers from the Internet to make things running better. Dumping your own headers might be time-consuming or a little chaotic, and you can also use the headers at https://github.com/theos/headers. Copy these headers to your $THEOS/include. Now let's start getting our hands dirty with tweak development.

Once Theos is installed properly, you can enter this command in your Terminal:

```
echo $THEOS
```

You should see the installation path of Theos on your terminal. Now let's start building our first tweak.

Once you have logged in to your device via SSH, you should create a folder in your home directory for keeping all your tweaks. For example, I created a folder named tweaks in my home directory.

Figure 6-20. *Initiating a tweak*

To initiate a new tweak, you enter the following bash command to open up the New Instance Creator:

```
$THEOS/bin/nic.pl
```

nic stands for New Instance Creator, which has some prefixed templates. You can also introduce some of your own templates according to your own preferences.

So before starting tweak development, you need to make sure you have a good grasp over Objective-C and C programming languages, as it involves a lot of coding in these two programming languages. In this chapter, we are writing simple hooks using minimal Objective-C code. Once you fire the NIC, you should see a screen with five options, which are just five basic templates bundled by default. Select option five for now, which will create a template tweak for you, followed by asking basic information that you need to fill in.

Once you create the tweak, you should see a folder in the tweaks directory you just created. You'll see a couple of files and folders in the directory, as shown in Figure 6-21.

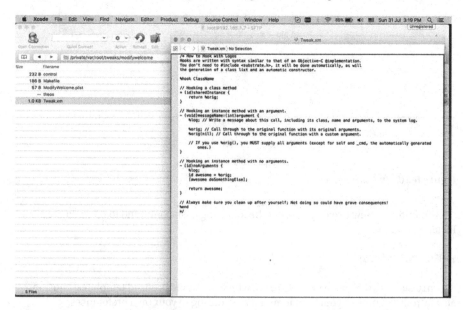

Figure 6-21. *Tweak files*

For now we will only work with Tweak.xm and the makefile. For the initial tweak we will make a tweak that hooks up the Springboard and creates a popup dialog upon launch. The objective of this tweak may be simple, but it will help you learn the basics of creating a tweak. So open Tweak.xm first. Since you are developing it in your device itself, you can use a text editor such as nano or use an app like Cyberduck, which connects via SFTB and lets you edit your files on your Mac's text editor. We will be using Xcode's editor with Cyberduck to write the code.

Once you connect to Cyberduck and open your tweak folder, you can instantly start editing the Tweak.xm file by selecting and clicking on edit. See Figure 6-22.

Figure 6-22. *Editing the Tweak.xm file*

When you open Tweak.xm, everything will be commented out with some instructions. For the basics, we will be just hooking up Springboard's applicationDidFinishLaunching method. A hook is declared using the %hook keyword and the block end is denoted using the %end keyword, as shown in Figure 6-22.

You need to make sure you follow the proper syntax or your Springboard will crash and might not launch. If your Springboard doesn't launch after the tweak, you can always take a SSH into your device and delete the tweak from the directory /Library/ MobileSubstrate/DynamicLibraries.

Let's hook up the method and execute some of the code in it. You need the Springboard header file, which we discussed earlier in the chapter, and you need to make sure you have your headers in your %THEOS/include folder. Otherwise this tweak won't compile.

This tweak is pretty simple. As shown in Figure 6-23, you are simply importing the header SpringBoard.h and hooking up the applicationDidFinishLaunching function. We call the UIAlertView method to create a popup dialog on the screen.

```
#import <SpringBoard/SpringBoard.h>

%hook SpringBoard

-(void)applicationDidFinishLaunching:(id)application {
%orig;

UIAlertView *alert = [[UIAlertView alloc] initWithTitle:@"iOS Penetration Testing"
message:@"Hello World , We are hooking up springboard"
delegate:nil
cancelButtonTitle:@"Close"
otherButtonTitles:nil];
[alert show];
[alert release];
}

%end
```

Figure 6-23. *The Tweak.xm file*

So that is it for the Tweak.xm file. Now we need to modify the makefile a bit to finally compile our first tweak.

We just need to add the necessary frameworks. In this case, as we are using UIAlertView, we need to add the UIKit framework. If you are running the tweak on a 64-bit device, you should add the first line ARCHS = amrv7 arm64, which defines the supported architectures, as shown in Figure 6-24.

■ **Note** UIAlertView triggers a popup to display a message to the users.

```
ARCHS = armv7 arm64
include theos/makefiles/common.mk

TWEAK_NAME = welcomeModified
welcomeModified_FILES = Tweak.xm
welcomeModified_FRAMEWORKS = UIKit
include $(THEOS_MAKE_PATH)/tweak.mk


after-install::
install.exec "killall -9 SpringBoard"
```

Figure 6-24. The makefile

So that is it for the code part. Now let's compile our tweak and run it. Compiling it is pretty straightforward; all you need to do is go to the particular directory in your Terminal and type `make package install`. After that, your device should do a soft reboot because of the last line in the makefile. See Figure 6-25.

Figure 6-25. Compiling the tweak

And now upon reboot, you should be welcomed by a `UIAlertView` that's generated from our tweak, as shown in Figure 6-26.

Figure 6-26. *UIAlertView*

As you can see in Figure 6-26, the tweak triggered a `UIAlertView` displaying the message we specified. Writing a tweak isn't too difficult in this case, as the goal was very simple. However, writing some serious tweaks that have a lot of functionalities will require more development effort.

Let's learn how we can write a tweak for a specific application. Since we have used DVIA for all our testing, we will be again writing a tweak for it. We will take up the same runtime manipulation that requires us to bypass the login challenge. In the previous chapters, you learned how to bypass the login, so you know what you need to do. Essentially, you need to change the isLoginValidated method in the RuntimeManipulationDetailsVC view controller to return YES (true). The technique will be the same here, but we need to make sure that we add the bundle of DVIA only in the makefile, while creating the tweak so that we only hook the DVIA app. We will then write a hook as a tweak and change the value of the isLoginValidated method of RuntimeManipulationDetailsVC to return YES. That will create the tweak.

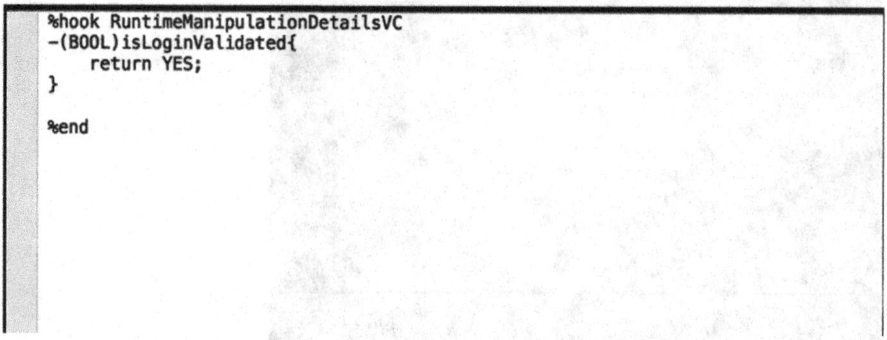

```
%hook RuntimeManipulationDetailsVC
-(BOOL)isLoginValidated{
    return YES;
}

%end
```

Figure 6-27. The DVIA tweak

The makefile of this tweak is going to be almost same, but we don't need to add any framework in this tweak. The Tweak.xm file is also very simple, as you can see in Figure 6-28.

Figure 6-28. The login bypass

That's it. Now we can compile this tweak the same way we did in the previous example. If you have opted for killing the Springboard, the device will under go a soft reboot and when you open up your DVIA and tap the login panel, the login screen will be bypassed, as expected from our tweak.

So this completes a very high-level introduction to iOS tweak development. For more examples or to get further inspiration or ideas about tweaks, you may explore some of the tweaks for real-world apps and the iOS operating system itself at repositories like "Bigboss Repo" on Cydia.

Summary

This descriptive chapter took you through various utilities provided by iRET and IDB, which are equally good and important tools for iOS penetration testing. It's a good idea to go through all the utilities provided for a better understanding. Tweak development is a very broad topic and we only cover a part of it here. You'll likely have more creative and useful ideas for tweak development when you start developing different iOS tweaks.

In the next chapter, we talk about the defense mechanism, which can be used in iOS application development, including the best security practices.

CHAPTER 7

■ ■ ■

iOS App Security Practices

So far it has been a journey of testing, configuring, decompiling, and debugging the iOS apps. You have worked on different methodologies and techniques for penetrating into an iOS application. In this last chapter, we talk about securing iOS apps according to the best practices and industry standards. We all know that perfect security is an illusion; however, there is a lot we can do with our app to make sure we make it hard for someone to attack or play around with it. This chapter talks about best practices for storing data, communicating with the server, deploying apps on the App Store, and other methods to make sure we give our best to secure the application. We will be thinking like a security conscious app developer and a penetration tester at the same time to ensure we develop the application from both point of views.

As a developer, we need to make sure the app is functional and production ready. On the other hand, it is to be developed with a penetration tester's perspective, making sure attacks cannot be easily carried out on the app and that the user data is secured and safe.

We discussing different aspects of the application architecture, including the basic small issues a lot of developer skip in their applications. Often, a lot of developers use plists or NSUserDefaults for storing confidential data, which is not a good idea. Because of this, a lot of the apps end up leaking confidential user data very easily.

■ **Tip** Keep an app handy for practice and apply the methods and tools discussed in this chapter for a better understanding.

Storage in iOS

iOS as an OS provides a lot of options to store user data suiting different needs. However, we as developers need to ensure we use the best available resource depending on our particular need with data safety in mind. Client-side data storage is not very safe, as it can always be tampered with. Sensitive data should be stored in cases only when it is really needed and no other option is available. You also need to ensure it is encrypted and stored in a safe place. So for an iOS application, you should ensure the following four points are taken care of:

- Data in transit is protected
- Authenticity of people accessing the data is confirmed

- User personal identifiable information is kept safe
- Untrusted files and data are kept with care

Data Storage Security

User data is the most crucial part of the application so you need to make sure that the user data is stored in a secured storage. iOS has a couple of options for storing user data using NSUserDefault, plists, CoreData framework, and keychain. We have already studied the security of these options to store user data. A very common mistake that a lot of developers do is store credentials in NSUserDefault and plist files, as it is not encrypted. However if you really want to store confidential data in CoreData, you can use this library https://github.com/project-imas/encrypted-core-data, which is based on the famous SQLCipher extension for encryption of SQLite databases. You can check out the Git repo of SQLCipher at https://github.com/sqlcipher/sqlcipher, which provides a guide on configuring SQLCipher for your application.

■ **Note**   SQLCipher is an SQLite extension that provides 256-bit AES encryption of database files.

For sensitive data, keychain is an encrypted service that can reliably store use data. It looks like a reliable solution for keeping user data safely. You can consider saving your private encrypted data in keychain, as shown in Table 7-1. Moreover, you should be very clear with file data protection classes in iOS and use them wisely.

Table 7-1. *Keychain Data Protection Comparison*

Availability	File Data Protection	Keychain Data Protection
When Unlocked	NSFileProtectionComplete	kSecAttrAccessibleWhen Unlocked
When Locked	NSFileProtectionComplete UnlessOpen	N/A
After First Unlock	NSFileProtectionCompleteUntil FirstUserAuthentication	kSecAttrAccessibleAfter FirstUnlock
Always	NSFileProtectionNone	kSecAttrAccessibleAlways
Passcode enabled	N/A	kSecAttrcAccessibleWhen PasscodeSetThisDeviceOnly

If you want to learn more about iOS data protection and understand file data protection, you can check out more insights about it at https://www.apple.com/business/docs/iOS_Security_Guide.pdf. You can also use obfuscation and encryption for one more layer of security of the data. For that, you can use https://github.com/RNCryptor/RNCryptor, which provides an AES-256 encryption wrapper for iOS.

■ **Note**   *Obfuscation* is an intended act of making a communication or a part of data confusing, thereby making it harder for people to understand. *Encryption* is a way of encoding data in such a way that it is accessible only to the authorized people using a key or a secret password.

You can download RNCryptor for Swift and Objective-C depending on the platform you are developing your iOS application with. Figure 7-1 shows an example of its implementation in Swift; you can easily get the documentation for Objective-C. You should always consider using it for storing usernames and passwords in local storage rather than storing them in plaintext. The public GitHub repository of RNCryptor has very good documentation for using the library. You should consider going through all of it before using it. It can be easily installed using CocoaPods in your project.

■ **Note**   CocoaPods is the dependency manager for Swift and Objective-C Cocoa projects and has around 23,000 libraries.

```swift
// Encryption
let data: NSData = ...
let password = "My Secret"
let ciphertext = RNCryptor.encryptData(data, password: password)

// Decryption
do {
    let originalData = try RNCryptor.decryptData(ciphertext, password: password)
    // ...
} catch {
    print(error)
}
```

Figure 7-1. RNCryptor implementation in Swift

Apart from the data storage security, here are few other best practices for secure coding that developers should always follow while developing an app:

- Always use text fields with secure options that obfuscate the text once it's typed, thereby allowing the users to safely type confidential data like passwords, PINs, and so on.

- Store user authentication tokens in keychain, which encrypts the data before storing it, thereby ensuring the authentication token is safe and only accessible to the application whenever needed.

- UIWebViews should be avoided, as they introduce web-based vulnerabilities like XSS, HTML injection, etc. in your application.

- The application's Pasteboard should be cleared once the application goes in background mode, ensuring it's only accessible within the application.

- Enable PIEs (position-independent executables), as they are a body of code that can be loaded and run from anywhere in virtual memory and thus do no need to be loaded at a fixed address. This makes it harder for someone to write an exploit code for the application.

- Disable NSLog in release mode, thereby ensuring that the application doesn't fill up space with log messages and doesn't reveal any confidential data in the logs.

- Use NSURLScheme to send non-confidential data, because private data that's being used to facilitate NSURLScheme might lead to a vulnerability.

Transport Layer Security

The transport layer is one of the most crucial components of data security and the most attacked layer, as it deals with exchanging the app's data between the client and the server. Man-in-the-middle attacks are a common attack vector, and they allow attackers to sneak into client-server communication and modify the data on transit for fun and profit. However, most of the time, people ensure the communication from client to server is encrypted but attackers still manage a way to subvert that encrypted communication by installing their own root certificates. In this section, we first discuss Apple's App Transport Security and then talk about certificate pinning.

App Transport Security was introduced in iOS 9 and assumingly in watchOS 2.0, which by default, doesn't allow unencrypted and weakly encrypted communication traffic into the device and thereby enforces an extra layer of security in the iOS apps. Although it can be explicitly turned off, it has some really good checks to only allow fully encrypted data to be exchanged between the app and its server. App Transport Security actively encourages use of best practices while communicating from the app to the server, the most basic one being using HTTPS instead of HTTP. Apart from that, here are the other standard checks in ATS:

- Server must at least support Transport Layer Security (TLS) 1.2 (see https://www.ietf.org/rfc/rfc5246.txt)

- Certificates must be signed with SHA256 or better with at least 2048 bits for RSA or 256 bits for Elliptic curve keys (see https://www.ssl.com/guide/ssl-best-practices-a-quick-and-dirty-guide/)

Connection ciphers must provide *forward secrecy* (see https://en.wikipedia.org/wiki/Forward_secrecy).

■ **Note**   *Forward secrecy* is a property of secure communications that ensures that compromise of long-term keys doesn't affect past session keys and protects past sessions against future compromise of keys or passwords.

So you must ensure you follow these guidelines before purchasing your SSL certificate. You can also use https://letsencrypt.org for getting SSL certificates for your server, which is a free service and has been backed up by giants like Mozilla, Cisco, Google, etc. Installing SSL certificate with the given guidelines is just one part of the problem. Attackers can bypass by installing their own root certificates from tools like Burp and Charles Proxy and can still view the traffic. To counter this, there is technique called SSL certificate pinning, which we will discuss next.

Certificate Pinning

Certificate pinning is a technique of client0server secured communication. It works by trusting only known entities and rejects communication with non-trusted entities. In this method, the public key fingerprint of the app's server is hard-coded into the client (in our case, the app) and the app will reject negotiation with the server if there's a mismatch. Certificate pinning is an amazing technique to keep out a lot of malicious attackers and script kiddies as it makes MITM almost impossible to execute without jailbreaking the device. It is a simple method of adding another layer of security on the top of SSL. However, it should be implemented properly by ensuring proper SSL configuration or you may end up locking up yourself from communicating with the server. In iOS, AFNetworking library supports certificate pinning and it is quite easy to integrate the protection in existing apps (see https://infinum.co/the-capsized-eight/articles/how-to-make-your-ios-apps-more-secure-with-ssl-pinning).

SSL pinning (see Figure 7-2) is a method for making sure that the client checks the authenticity of the server against known copies of certificates. SSL pinning is an ideal solution for ensuring reliable client-server communication on mobile apps, as they communicate with a limited number of servers, making it feasible to incorporate it in that environment. Popular apps like Twitter, Snapchat, and Google Chrome have started implementing this technique in their applications.

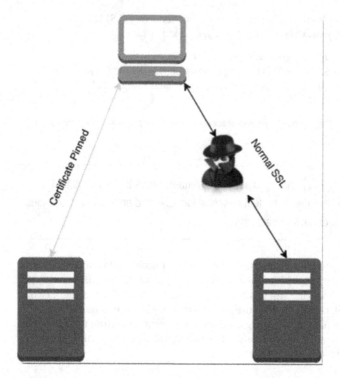

Figure 7-2. *SSL Pinning*

SSL pinning can be bypassed on jailbroken devices using tools like iOS SSL Kill Switch (see `https://github.com/iSECPartners/ios-ssl-kill-switch`). It is an application for jailbroken devices that helps bypass this certificate validation check on runtime, but it is still suggested as it makes intruding harder for attackers and is a good check against script kiddies.

Now let's see a simple implementation of SSL pinning on an iOS application.

All you need to do is bundle the app with a known list of certificates and make sure that every network request goes through the validation process and is dropped if the certificate validation fails. Here is the method used for implementing SSL pinning inside the `NSURLConnectionDelegate` protocol.

`connection:willSendRequestForAuthenticationChallenge:`

The Objective-C code shown in Figure 7-3 is an example of performing SSL pinning.

```
- (void)connection:(NSURLConnection *)connection
    willSendRequestForAuthenticationChallenge:(NSURLAuthenticationChallenge *)challenge
{
    SecTrustRef serverTrust = challenge.protectionSpace.serverTrust;
    SecCertificateRef certificate = SecTrustGetCertificateAtIndex(serverTrust, 0);
    NSData *remoteCertificateData =
        CFBridgingRelease(SecCertificateCopyData(certificate));
    NSString *cerPath = [[NSBundle mainBundle] pathForResource:@"MyLocalCertificate"
        ofType:@"cer"];
    NSData *localCertData = [NSData dataWithContentsOfFile:cerPath];
    if ([remoteCertificateData isEqualToData:localCertData]) {
        NSURLCredential *credential = [NSURLCredential credentialForTrust:serverTrust];
        [[challenge sender] useCredential:credential forAuthenticationChallenge:
            challenge];
    }
    else {
        [[challenge sender] cancelAuthenticationChallenge:challenge];
    }
}
```

Figure 7-3. Implementing SSL Pinning

Implementing SSL pinning is not really difficult; however, it can be easily bypassed in jailbroken devices, thus you should make sure that you send useful data only with all these layers of security from client to the server. A common practice of developers is to implement SSL pinning and jailbreak detection in a combination and terminate the application when the jailbroken device is detected. However, there are many ways of bypassing jailbreak detection, as you saw in earlier chapters. A good combination of few jailbreak detection mechanisms and SSL pinning will make a good defense strategy for less motivated attackers. Always remember that it is good to make the attack process as difficult as possible, because the harder it gets, the more people lose motivation to attack your application.

Anti-Debugging Protections

This technique is used by a lot of developers to prevent attackers from attaching debuggers to the app on runtime, which is used to analyze and modify the app behavior. We will discuss the most used method of preventing attackers from the attaching debugger.

ptrace with PT_DENY_ATTACH

ptrace is a system call used to observe and control the execution of another process via breakpoint debugging and system call tracing. It is called as follows:

int ptrace(int request,pid_t pid, caddr_t addr,int data);

In this call, the first argument (request) specifies the action that needs to be performed. One of the operations is called PT_DENY_ATTACH with the value of 31 informing the operating system that it doesn't want to get traced or debugged. However, in case of any trace/debug attempt, the operating system denies this, making the debugger unable to attach to the particular process.

The code shown in Figure 7-4 will prevent GDB from attaching to the application process.

```
int main(int argc, char **argv)
{
        ptrace(PT_DENY_ATTACH, 0, 0, 0);
        printf("Sorry You Cannot Attach a debugger now");
        while (1)
            {
                    sleep(1);
                    printf(".");
                    fflush(stdout);
            }
        return 0;
}
```

Figure 7-4. Anti-debugger implementation

An attacker might still be able to get around this. Getting away with this is quite easy for an attacker by easily modifying the arguments in ptrace itself, but again it is a good way of adding layers of security to your application.

You should also follow the Apple Security guide available publicly at https://developer.apple.com/library/ios/documentation/Security/Conceptual/SecureCodingGuide/Introduction.html as a reference while developing your native iOS applications. Make sure that your backend web services are designed with security in mind. Follow the OWASP guide on web service security https://www.owasp.org/index.php/Web_Service_Security_Cheat_Sheet, which will give you insight into developing secure and robust web services for communication from your client to the server.

Secure Development Guidelines

This section contains a consolidated checklist of security best practices. These are the things you need to make sure of before rolling out your app to the public. Make sure all these guidelines are taken care of so that the app has a standard security setup. This will make it harder for people to attack it.

Untrusted Data

"Never trust user data" is a wise saying in the field of information security. Doing so this will leave you vulnerable to exploitation of entry points. User data should, ideally, be input-filtered and output-escaped, depending on the context. Applications accept input from the users in many ways and at many places, so they should always make sure not to implicitly trust the input from the users and always filter it for special characters.

Otherwise, your applications are prone to client-side cross-site scripting and SQLInjections, which can be really dangerous for your application while using UIWebViews. Input sanitization strips out potentially harmful characters from the user input using *blacklist methods,* which include stripping out the data on the basis of a predefined list, and *whitelist methods,* which include only accepting a particular format of data.

Session Management

User session management is another important security-oriented component in any application and you need to be very diligent about managing user session securely. User sessions (in the form OAuth tokens, etc.) should be encrypted and stored in keychain. It should be renewed often so that in the event of breach, the effect is not long lasting. Session keys or auth tokens generation should be based on a combination of different relevant entities. A single UDID (Unique Device Identifier) found in every device or something similar should not be linked to a particular user, as this can always be faked by an attacker.

▓ **Note**   The user session is a mechanism used in client-server communication to keep track of a particular user's activity and uniquely identify a particular user.

Data Storage

As already discussed, user data should be encrypted and stored in appropriate places and private data should be stored in the keychain. Always remember that client data should never be stored on the device except when there is no alternative.

Geolocation Handling

You should always be very careful about using geolocation data and should use the least degree of accuracy while fetching user-location data. Also make sure you gracefully handle the locationServicesEnabled and authorizationStatus method responses, making sure user geolocation data is kept safely. You should never store user logs locally and anonymize user data logging to your server; otherwise, privacy concerns might be raised by the app users.

Escape Classic C Attacks

Always check for classic C vulnerabilities arising due to using common vulnerable C functions resulting from buffer overflows. Remember to format the strings in your application. Make sure you specify the exact format of the string. For example:

```
Char *someVar;
someVar = "%x%x%x%x%x%x"
printf(someVar);
```

This is one of the most common vulnerabilities, where a variable is directly passed to `printf()` without specifying a format string. However, in real world, the input string might come from user input and would be carefully crafted code that could exploit a buffer overflow vulnerability. A better version of the previous code is:

```
Char *someVar;
someVar = "%x%x%x%x%x%x"
printf("%s",someVar);
```

This version will literally print %x%x%x%x%x%x, treating it as a string rather than as a special character.

Transport Layer

Your application and server should always communicate securely over HTTPS and you should also perform a manual check on the SSL. This guide can be really helpful when doing this: http://www.exploresecurity.com/wp-content/uploads/custom/SSL_manual_cheatsheet.html.

Static analyzers are tools or plugins that either integrate with the IDE or run stand-alone to analyze the source code and find vulnerabilities in the application's code. You can use the native static code analyzer in Xcode by selecting Product ➤ Analyze, as shown in Figure 7-5.

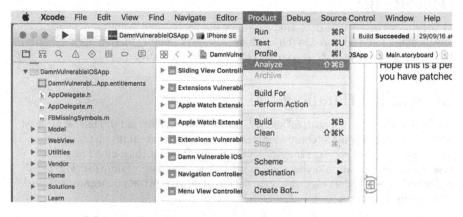

Figure 7-5. *Validating code using static code analyzer*

The static code analyzer will parse your projects' source code and identify issues like memory management flaws, unused variables, API usage flaws, dereferencing null pointers, and so on.

Closing Thoughts

We have finally come to the end of this journey of getting into iOS reverse engineering and penetration testing. This industry is continuously evolving with new attack vectors as well as new open source and commercial mobile app security tools and techniques. To make the most of this book, you should follow the tutorials provided in the book as well as explore the issues more. However, there are few things you need to work on quite a bit—reverse engineering is one of them. iOS assembly needs a lot of background work as well, so make sure you spend a lot of time on your disassembler getting the most of it. iOS development and testing is a very huge domain, so you should get very clear with Objective-C and the base of C to understand the low-level APIs used in many applications, which tend to have security vulnerabilities.

Make sure you follow these guidelines before sending your application in testing mode. The application should also go through blackbox penetration test before you release it to the public.

This book serves as an introductory base into iOS penetration testing and reverse engineering. Upon completion of this book, you should do some deeper dives into these tools and platforms and practice as much as possible to get comfortable. You should also ask a lot of questions at the appropriate forums to get clearer insights into iOS penetration testing and reverse engineering. You should also follow the OWASP guide on secure development and SDLC specific to iOS development. Apple also has a secure coding guide that you can look at. Read this guide and make sure you follow them at https://www.apple.com/business/docs/iOS_Security_Guide.pdf.

Index

A

Address Space Layout Randomization (ASLR), 3
Anti-debugging protections, 125–126
Application delegate protocol, 63
ApplicationDidFinishLaunching function, 113
App transport security, 6
Authentication, 45
Authorization, 45
Automating app testing
    manual penetration, 97
    repetitive tasks, 97

B

Binary Analysis Results tab, 106
Binary analyzing, 101
Binary button, 100
Blackbox testing
    definition, 47
    intercepting network traffic,
        (*see* Network interception)
    iOS applications, 47
    runtime analysis
        application icon, 65
        aprogramming experience, 61
        class-dump, 67
        classRuntimeManipulation DetailsVC, 70
        controller's class, 68
        Cycript, 62
        Cycript interpreter, 70
        Cycript's capabilities, 65
        DVIA app, 66
        DVIA login, 70
        gswizzling library, 62

JavaScript syntax, 63
login bypass, 66
LoginValidated method, 71
NSString type, 69
objective-C code, 64
Read Tutorial button, 67
SFTP client, 67
status bar, 64
URL string, 69
URL variable, 68
username/password combination, 70–71
Blocking installed apps detection, 6
Boot procedure, 4–5
Brute force technique, 6
Buffer overflows, 40–41

C

Certificate pinning, 123
Client-side injection, 44
Cocoa framework, 22
CocoaPods, 22, 121
Cocoa Touch, 1
Code signing method, 2
Control Flow Graph (CFG), 76
Core OS layer, 7
Cyberduck, 112
Cycript installation, 37–38

D, E

Damn Vulnerable iOS application (DVIA), 54–55
Data Execution Prevention (DEP), 3
Data storage security, 120–122

Get the eBook for only $4.99!

Why limit yourself?

Now you can take the weightless companion with you wherever you go and access your content on your PC, phone, tablet, or reader.

Since you've purchased this print book, we are happy to offer you the eBook for just $4.99.

Convenient and fully searchable, the PDF version enables you to easily find and copy code—or perform examples by quickly toggling between instructions and applications.

To learn more, go to http://www.apress.com/us/shop/companion or contact support@apress.com.

Printed in the United States
By Bookmasters